SIMPLY CHINESE FEASTS

BY SUZIE LEE

SIMPLY CHINESE FEASTS

Tasty Recipes for Friends and Family

Hardie Grant

BOOKS

CONTENTS

INTRODUCTION

Growing up I was extremely fortunate to be surrounded by food. I spent my childhood looking forward to the next family gathering because all my relatives in Northern Ireland owned a Chinese takeaway, meaning there were few sociable hours, and us children had to wait for the next birthday party or major festival/celebration to meet up and play! Our family gatherings were not modest in size – at any given moment, there would have been an average of 30 people and even 40-plus if all the cousins came along.

My parents were very traditional, following all the traditions they were brought up with in Hong Kong and continuing them when they started their own family with the five of us. I am grateful for the importance they placed on celebrating significant festivals, which always centred around food.

Holidays are essential to Chinese culture, and Chinese family gatherings centred around feasts and festivals were just another reason to eat and be together.

CHINESE HERITAGE AND TRADITIONS

I am going to give you a quick whistlestop tour of my favourite Chinese celebrations and the foods associated with each festival. Each one is a feast. The Chinese follow and believe in many customs and these are matched with food.

Birthdays, the Mid-Autumn Festival and Chinese New Year were my absolute favourite feasts!

Chinese culture is heavily based around the worship of Heaven and Earth, and lots of festivals held throughout the year follow the traditional lunar calendar. Harvest in the different seasons is a cause for celebration in the form of festivals, including the Mid-Autumn Festival (aka the Mooncake Festival) and the Dragon Boat Festival.

CHINESE NEW YEAR

Chinese New Year (aka the Lunar New Year and Chinese Spring Festival) begins on the first day of the new moon of the first lunar month each year. In a lunar calendar year there are 13 months; therefore the actual date of Chinese New Year is different each year. But it always falls between 21st January and 20th February and lasts for seven days.

There are over 4,000 years of history, myths and legends behind the Chinese New Year stories and they are fascinating, especially the repeating 12 animal Chinese zodiac cycle. This is believed to have begun with the Jade Emperor of the Qin dynasty where 'The Great Race' started and the order in which the animals arrived determined their place in the zodiac. This is the order in which the zodiac animals arrived – Rat, Ox, Tiger, Rabbit, Dragon, Snake, Horse, Goat, Monkey, Rooster, Dog and Pig.

I was born on the 17th September 1983. The Chinese zodiac splits into other elements, and I am a 'water pig', which I think actually rings quite true for me! I am at one in the water and used to swim for Ulster, and I am also very stubborn. Maybe some generalisations and coincidences, but I'll take it! Haha!

Here are some of the things I remember vividly while growing up in a very superstitious household with my Mum during Chinese New Year:

1. Cleaning the house like mad, opening the windows and making sure you brush all the bad luck out the back door (NEVER through the front door)!

2. Buying in a truckload of mandarin oranges to give to people. You also receive them in return because when you give the mandarin oranges (in a pair) to guests in Cantonese it is pronounced *shung gum* which literally means 'giving gold'. So for the Chinese this is a symbol of presenting prosperity and good luck to the recipient. It's also traditional to bath in mandarin peels and pomelo leaves to bring luck the night before (never, ever wash or cut your hair or shower on Chinese New Year's Day, as you will be washing away any luck you had!).

3. Exchanging red envelopes filled with money, which means giving blessings of wealth and good fortune. This was an extremely exciting time because your money box was always bulging with many people coming to visit us and my family is quite extensive!

4. DO NOT BUY NEW SHOES in this period ... the word for shoes in Cantonese sounds like 'rough', so yet again another bad luck omen.

DRAGON BOAT FESTIVAL

The Dragon Boat Festival falls on the fifth day of the fifth lunar month and marks a change in the weather in China. It was originally believed that the waters were ruled by the dragon who controlled rainfall. The fifth month is just before the summer rainy season and therefore people offered sacrifices to the dragon to stop the rain flooding crops and killing livestock. The food associated with this festival is known as *zongzi*, which are glutinous rice dumplings filled with ingredients such as marinaded pork, salted duck egg yolks, mushrooms and chestnuts and then wrapped in bamboo leaves. This is a labour-intensive dish and family members usually gather around to make it together. I remember helping my Mum and auntie fill the parcels. I would tie the string around the rice dumplings badly, so my Mum always had to tighten it for me. When I was growing up, I was told that the rice bundles were thrown into the waters to feed the dragon, but there are many different versions of this tale. Centuries later, these delicious rice parcels were deemed too delicious to throw in the water, and so to commemorate the occasion the dragon boat race began people now eat the zongzi. Hong Kong has an extremely famous dragon boat race, which takes place in Victoria Harbour in Tsim Sha Tsui.

MID-AUTUMN FESTIVAL

The Mid-Autumn Festival is also known as the Mooncake Festival, and is celebrated on the 15th day of the eighth month of the lunar year when the moon is shining at its brightest and fullest. In Chinese culture the moon is pivotal to many festivals/holidays, and so the festival was used to worship the moon and give thanks for the summer harvest. I grew up running around the garden with colourful candlelit paper lanterns after eating a gigantic feast of 'all the good stuff', including mooncakes. Mooncakes were created as an offering to the moon and are traditionally filled with a sweet lotus seed paste and either one or two salted duck egg yolks to represent the moon (this is typical of a popular Hong Kong mooncake).

WEDDINGS

I have been to many a Chinese wedding, and these are big food affairs. They are my definition of a banquet of endless eating – which I never complained about! There were at least eight courses because the word for 'eight' in Chinese sounds like good luck. Dishes such as lobster signify joy and completeness and a whole fish signifies plenty. Other must-haves on the banquet menu are chicken, suckling roast pig, crab claws, soup, rice and noodles.

A part of the Chinese wedding traditions is the tea ceremony where the bride and groom serve tea to their respective families out of respect and gratitude. At my own wedding I blended some Chinese and Western traditions together. I was grateful to be able to do this and follow tradition in both 'my worlds'.

HOW TO USE THIS BOOK

Compiling the recipes for this book was a lot of fun, as it was filled with great memories of feasting at different occasions as a child. Below, I have gathered the recipes into six 'feasts' – Birthday, Chinese New Year, Dai Pai Dong, Dim Sum, Family Feasts and Takeaway.

Use these groupings as a guide to plan your menu. However, as I have said, this is only a guide and you can mix and match and cross over dishes from the different groupings. So, create your own feast depending on your mood.

BIRTHDAY

Having a seven-member family, birthdays were always fun, never mind when you add in the extended family. I loved birthday parties because we enjoyed treats we usually never got regularly like cream soda with milk. Don't knock this until you try it, especially if you like ice cream floats! The recipes grouped here are really special ones made by my Mum, such as her unique 'fruit salad', and writing that recipe in particular got me quite emotional.

CHINESE NEW YEAR

I am always jealous of my big sister Angela who lives in Hong Kong now with her family because she has an extensive range of dishes to eat during Chinese New Year which are easy to come by. These recipes are my stand out family favourites, but also I have showcased different food groups as there is massive significance to what is served at Chinese New Year. For example, seafood is auspicious and therefore it is good luck to eat it during Chinese New Year. Noodles are always served as they represent a wish for a long life.

DAI PAI DONG

These are a gathering of street-market food stalls. In Tai Po, Hong Kong, where my Dad's side of the family grew up, there was a huge *dai pai dong*, which has now turned into a very modern affair. So many different types of foods to try and eat on the go, it really was a 360-degree sensory experience.

DIM SUM

I love dim sum and it reminds me of our holidays in Hong Kong, which has the best dim sum with all the dim sum carts going round the massive restaurants. The variety is colossal, but with each portion being mainly bite-sized pieces you could always try lots of dishes (which we always did as a family). My children enjoy dim sum now and I love introducing them to my favourites – they have become really addicted to all the bread-based dishes, so in this menu I have modified the recipes to suit the home kitchen.

FAMILY FEASTS

Every Monday night Mum was off work and we got to sit down together properly and eat. This might have been any dish, but my combination of recipes in this menu strongly features my home comfort food and what I feed my own family now regularly.

TAKEAWAY

I could not leave this menu out of the book since the number of people who contact me for takeaway (takeout) recipes is quite astonishing. I have included my husband's favourite kung po chicken and the highly sought after salted chilli chicken. Having been brought up in my family takeaway, these recipes are close to my heart and provide another small glimpse into my upbringing.

STAPLE INGREDIENTS

FRESH

Root ginger (fresh or frozen)

Onions

Garlic (fresh or frozen)

Spring onions (scallions)

Chillies

Eggs

Vegetables

SEASONING

Light and dark soy sauce

Toasted sesame oil

Oyster sauce or vegetarian stir-fry sauce

Shaoxing wine

Rice wine vinegar

Black sesame oil

Dried fermented black beans

Brown sauce

Ketchup

Chilli oil

Black vinegar

Peanut butter

Vegetable oil

Fine sea salt

White pepper

Black pepper

Sesame oil

Chinese five-spice powder (cinnamon, cloves, fennel, star anise, Szechuan peppercorns)

Chicken or vegetable stock powder

Caster (superfine) and granulated sugar

Stock cubes

Fermented red bean curd/tofu

DRY (BACK-UP)

Onion powder/granules

Garlic powder/granules

Chilli (hot pepper) powder/flakes

Ground ginger

Dried shiitake mushrooms

Sesame seeds (white, black or both)

Peanuts

Wood ear mushrooms

Dried prawns (shrimp)

Lap cheong (Chinese cured sausage)

Evaporated milk

Condensed milk

OTHER

Basmati rice

Noodles (rice, egg, glass)

Cornflour (cornstarch)

Rice flour

Milk

Milk powder

Plain (all-purpose) flour

Spam

Wheat starch

Wonton wrappers

Spring roll wrappers

Choot choi (tinned/vacuum-packed, pickled snow cabbage), or pickled Chinese cabbage (slightly chunkier)

MUST-HAVE EQUIPMENT

There are a few must-have items that will help you on this *Simply Chinese* cooking journey, and I therefore feel are worth the investment.

WOK

You do not have to buy an expensive non-stick wok. The key to making a stainless-steel, aluminium or cast-iron wok non-stick is to 'season' it. To do this, use some paper towel to rub vegetable or sunflower oil over the inside of the wok, so the whole surface has a light coating of oil. Heat the wok slowly on the stove-top until it is smoking and then wipe thoroughly with more paper towel. Repeat the oiling, heating and wiping process until the paper towel comes away clean. The wok will blacken and lose its silver colour. It is now seasoned and you have given your wok wok hay, which means 'energy or breath of the wok'.

METAL SIEVE

Use to strain noodles, blanch vegetables and remove excess food fragments from oil if deep-frying.

STEAMER

Use a steamer, or a large pan with a lid into which you can fit a trivet stand, steam rack and heatproof dish.

TONGS

Used to extract food from woks and pots and for mixing and stirring.

MEASURING JUGS, SPOONS AND SCALES

These items are important for the precision required in the recipes.

CHOPSTICK ETIQUETTE

1. Do cross chopsticks over – it's bad luck.

2. Do not have chopsticks sticking up from your bowl – this resembles incense sticks in a grave.

3. Do not use your personal chopsticks to pick up communal food – there will be communal chopsticks (usually a different colour) set for each dish.

4. Do not point your chopsticks at anyone, wave them around or use them as drumsticks. These actions are highly disrespectful.

5. Do not skewer your food with your chopsticks; use the chopsticks to grip the food, while also lifting the bowl as you eat.

KEY INGREDIENTS, TERMS AND TIPS

You will find that I use some methods, terms and ingredients frequently throughout the book and I thought it would be helpful to pull them all together and explain them fully here.

CORNFLOUR

I love cornflour (cornstarch) because it is such a versatile ingredient that can be used in the following ways:

VELVETING Add cornflour to meat marinades. As the meat cooks, the cornflour acts as a barrier, helping to keep moisture in and the meat juicy.

BINDING Cornflour binds ingredients together in recipes such as the Traditional Dumplings on page 126.

CRISPING Used to help form a crispy exterior when deep- or pan-frying foods – for example, see Kung Po Chicken on page 50.

NOODLES Cornflour gives noodles a slightly translucent quality.

THICKENER Use cornflour to create a paste for thickening soups and sauces. Cornflour paste is the key sauce thickener in all Chinese cooking. It is made by combining cornflour and water at a ratio of 1:2. Mix together 1 tablespoon of cornflour and 2 tablespoons of cold or cooled water in a bowl until fully combined. Do not use hot water as this will create a lumpy mixture. Remember to give the mixture a stir before using, as the cornflour will have settled to the bottom of the bowl.

BLANCHING AND PARBOILING MEAT

This is always done in Chinese cooking. Put the meat in a saucepan of cold water and bring it to the boil to allow the impurities to float to the surface. This helps reduce excess fat in the meat and removes blood from the bones and the taste of gaminess from the meat, which it might add to the dish. It also ensures the broth or soup you are making with the meat will be very clear. I hate waste, so I don't throw away the water in which the meat was boiled as it holds a lot of flavour. I just make sure the impurities and scum are scooped away with a sieve from the surface of the liquid.

STEAMING

This makes up a large part of my book. Steaming is a great way to cook vegetables, as it helps retain their nutrients, and is great for cooking meat and dumplings. So, if you do not have a steamer, I would highly recommend getting one!

SPLASH OF WATER

Always add a splash of water to vegetables when stir-frying to stop them from catching and burning in the wok.

SEAFOOD

01 一

海鮮

Fish is a very auspicious ingredient and symbolises the hope of receiving prosperity. There are certain rules for how the fish should be positioned: the head should be placed facing the most distinguished guests/elders out of respect. This person should eat the head first before the rest of the guests tuck in. The fish should also not be moved, while the two people facing the head and tail must drink together, as this is considered to have lucky connotations.

CHAPTER ONE

THE MENU

THE MENU

CRISPY SEA BREAM
20

LOBSTER NOODLES
22

FISH BALL
NOODLE SOUP
26

KING PRAWN EGGS
28

SCALLOPS WITH MUSHROOMS
AND PAK CHOI
31

CURRY FISH BALLS
AND DAIKON STEW
32

Crispy Sea Bream

SERVES: 4
PREP: 10 minutes
COOK: 20 minutes

Fish is a really auspicious food group and a whole fish is a must at banquets and special occasions. Mum used to make this, and I loved it: crunchy, salty, sweet fish skin against the tender fish meat – it was just delicious.

INGREDIENTS

fresh sea bream or other white whole fish, descaled, gutted and trimmed	500 g (1 lb 2 oz)
cornflour (cornstarch)	1 heaped tablespoon
vegetable oil	2 tablespoons
fresh ginger root, peeled and sliced into fine rounds	20 g (¾ oz)
Shaoxing wine	2 tablespoons

SAUCE

sugar	1 tablespoon
boiling water	3 tablespoons
light soy sauce	1½ tablespoons
white pepper	¼ teaspoon

METHOD

Ask your fishmonger to descale, gut and trim the fish, then clean by rinsing with water (you can sometimes buy the whole fish already prepared and cleaned at the supermarket). Dry the fish well with some paper towels to stop the oil spitting when frying. Dust the whole fish with the cornflour on both sides and set aside.

To make the sauce, dissolve the sugar in the water in a bowl, add the light soy sauce and pepper and mix together.

To cook the fish, heat the vegetable oil in a wok or large frying pan over a high heat. Add the ginger slices and fry for a couple of minutes until the ginger browns slightly at the edges. Remove the ginger and set aside.

Place the fish in the wok/pan and fry for 5 minutes (press down with a fish slice so the whole side is seared), then flip and repeat on the other side for a further 5 minutes. If the fish is starting to burn, lower the heat to medium and allow to cook for a couple of minutes longer on each side. You want the skin to have a lovely, golden, crunchy appearance.

Return the ginger slices to the pan/wok (you may need another tablespoon or so of oil to stop the fish sticking at this stage). Then drizzle the Shaoxing wine around the edges (not directly over the fish) and cook for about 1 minute.

Pour the prepared sauce around the fish, not directly over it. Allow the sauce to bubble and start to caramelise, then cook the fish for a couple of minutes on one side before flipping over and cooking on the other side. This will coat the fish in a sticky sauce. (If the sauce starts to burn, then add a splash of water.)

Slice into the fish to check it is fully cooked – the flesh should flake away from the bones. If not, cook for another couple of minutes. Plate up, ready for your feast.

TOP TIPS

- If there is any leftover fish, remove from the bone and use to bulk up a fried rice dish.

- Place the fish bones in a pot of water and boil down to make a stock.

Lobster Noodles

SERVES: 4
PREP: 30 minutes
COOK: 25 minutes

Lobster noodles are one of those decadent and delicious dishes that I crave. I'm always super excited to eat them when they're put in front of me! I have modified this recipe to include crispy, crunchy noodles instead of soft noodles, which is more characteristic of the dish, and provided instructions on using langoustines as well as lobster. This makes the recipe more cost-effective without compromising on flavour.

Langoustines are known in Ireland as scampi, but they are also called the Norway lobster because they are from the same family as lobsters. My kids LOVE this dish and I am so happy that I can create it easily.

INGREDIENTS

vegetable oil, for frying	
fresh ginger root, peeled and sliced into fine rounds	50 g (1¾ oz)
spring onions (scallions), white and green parts separated	6
Shaoxing wine	3 tablespoons

IF USING LOBSTER

fresh lobster	1 kg (2 lb 4 oz) (I used two lobsters)
plain (all-purpose) flour	2 tablespoons
cornflour (cornstarch) paste (p. 17)	1–2 tablespoons

IF USING LANGOUSTINE TAILS

langoustine tails	1 kg (2 lb 4 oz)

SAUCE

oyster sauce	4 tablespoons
chicken stock powder	½ tablespoon
white sugar	1 teaspoon
light soy sauce	2 teaspoons
water	150 ml (5 fl oz/ scant ⅔ cup)
cornflour (cornstarch) paste (p. 17)	1–2 tablespoons

NOODLES

fine egg noodle nests	4 x 25 g (1 oz)
vegetable oil, for frying	3 tablespoons

METHOD

Prepare the noodles by rehydrating in cold water for at least 30 minutes until the strands are separable, then drain, pat dry and leave on top of some paper towels to remove excess water. (You can use fresh egg noodles too, if you wish.)

If you are using lobster, see Preparing a Lobster (page 24) for how to split and cut into pieces. Then pat all the lobster pieces dry with some paper towels, dust the exposed flesh of the tail pieces in the cornflour and plain flour, and set aside.

If you are using langoustine tails, rinse thoroughly, then pat dry with paper towel.

To cook the lobster or langoustine tails, pour approximately 2 cm (¾ in) of vegetable oil into a wok or large frying pan, then place over a high heat. The oil is hot enough when it fizzes around the end of a wooden spoon.

IF YOU ARE USING LOBSTER

Shallow-fry in batches. The head will take around 5 minutes – flip at the halfway point to ensure it is evenly cooked. Remove the head with a metal spider or tongs and place on some paper towels to absorb the excess oil. Repeat for the claws, cooking for about 3 minutes and flipping halfway, and then the tails, which will also take around 3 minutes. The shell will change colour to a lovely, orangey red when the lobster pieces are cooked. Decant most of the oil, leaving approximately 2 tablespoons in the wok/pan.

IF YOU ARE USING LANGOUSTINE TAILS

Cook the langoustine tails in batches. Each batch will take around 5 minutes and the shells will turn a deeper orange/coral colour. The flesh will turn from opaque to white.

Now prepare to multi-task ... with the noodles in one pan and finishing the lobster or langoustines in another.

To cook the noodles, add the vegetable oil to a clean wok or large saucepan and heat to a high temperature. Put the air-dried noodles in the hot oil and press down with a fish slice into a flat dish shape in the wok/pan.

Fry the disc of noodles for about 3–4 minutes on each side until golden and crispy, then place a plate on top. Carefully flip the wok/pan and slide the uncooked side of the noodles back into the wok/pan. Fry for a further 3–4 minutes until golden and crisp. Then slide onto a serving dish.

Add the ginger and the white part of the spring onions to the same wok/pan you used for the lobster/langoustines, then fry off for about 1 minute until fragrant.

Return the lobster/langoustines to the wok/pan and toss the lovely, fragrant oil all over the shellfish pieces. Pour the Shaoxing wine around the edge of the wok/pan and toss all the ingredients through it.

To make the sauce, mix the oyster sauce, chicken stock powder, sugar and soy sauce together thoroughly in a bowl and add to the wok/pan along with the green part of the spring onions. Pour in the water and allow to bubble for a couple of minutes.

Next add a tablespoon of cornflour paste at a time and allow to thicken by bringing to a boil – the sauce should lightly coat all the lobster/langoustine pieces. This should take about 1 minute.

Now plate up, arranging the lobster/langoustine pieces decoratively over the crispy, crunchy noodles, and pour over the sauce.

TOP TIPS

- You can also use 750 g (1 lb 10 oz) lobster tails, but these are pricey!

- If you want to shorten the cooking time by at least 10 minutes, then instead of shallow frying the lobster/langoustine pieces, pour 500 ml (17 fl oz/generous 2 cups) of vegetable oil into a small cooking pot. Heat the oil and deep-fry each of the lobster pieces for about 30 seconds.

PREPARING A LOBSTER FOR COOKING

If you have bought the lobster from the fishmonger on the same day you plan to cook, ask them to help you prepare it by segmenting the head, two claws and body (cutting this into chunks).

Otherwise, when you get home, put the whole fresh lobster in the freezer for 20 minutes before cooking. When you are ready to cook, remove the lobster from the freezer.

Using a super-sharp knife, aim the point into the head between the eyes, then cut into the head with a swift downward motion. Then, feed a chopstick or knitting needle into the opening at the underside of the tail and through the body to ensure all the waste matter is removed, as it will drip out.

Remove each claw by twisting it off at the body, then use a claw/nut cracker or food mallet to crack each of the segments slightly, so they cook more evenly. Cut through the join at the neck to remove the head, then slice down the middle of the tail from the underside and chop each piece into large, bite-sized chunks. Repeat with the other lobster segments.

Fish Ball Noodle Soup

SERVES: 4
PREP: 20 minutes
COOK: 25 minutes

Having had conversations with my Dad for my cookbooks, I found out that this is his favourite thing to eat in Hong Kong! A bowl of fish ball noodle soup is so simple, but so tasty. Here, I show you how to make the fish balls from scratch, but you can also buy them from the fresh-and-frozen section in an Asian supermarket, which will save you even more time.

INGREDIENTS

NOODLES

ho fun noodles (or broad rice noodles)	400 g (14 oz)

FRESH FISH BALLS

skinned white fish or mackerel	500 g (1 lb 2 oz)
raw king prawns (shrimp), shelled and deveined	75 g (2½ oz)
sesame oil	1 teaspoon
egg white	30 g (1 oz) (about 1 small egg)
cornflour (cornstarch) paste (page 17)	1 tablespoon
salt	1½ tablespoons
white pepper	¾ teaspoon
iced water	75–100 ml (2½ oz/⅓ cup –3½ fl oz/scant ½ cup)

SOUP

water	1.5 litres (50 fl oz/6¼ cups)
fresh ginger root, peeled and sliced	30 g (1 oz)
spring onions (scallions), cut into 7.5 cm (3 in) chunks	30 g (1 oz)
chicken stock powder	1½ tablespoons
sesame oil	1 teaspoon
white pepper	¼ teaspoon
salt	

TO SERVE

blanched vegetables of your choice, such as broccoli, pak choi (bok choi) or Chinese cabbage, or chilli oil or soy sauce

TOP TIPS

- You can freeze the freshly made fish balls and they will keep for a month in the freezer.

- Use the fish balls in the Curry Fish Balls and Daikon Stew (page 32).

- Make your own ho fun noodles (found in my first book, *Simply Chinese,* page 114).

METHOD

Steep the noodles in boiling water for 3 minutes, then run under cold water and set aside.

To make the fish balls, place the fish and prawns in a food processor, then blitz together. Add the sesame oil, egg white, cornflour paste, ½ tablespoon of salt and the pepper, then blitz again.

Slowly pour in the iced water until the fish purée becomes smoother but not too fluid. You need to judge this by eye, so do not add all the iced water immediately. The process will take a couple of minutes and you are looking for a very thick, porridge-like consistency.

Fill a large basin or bowl with some hot water (not boiling) and another smaller bowl with tap water for rinsing your hands now and again.

Now here is the messy part. Take a handful of the fish mixture, then push it between your fingers and palm so it squeezes out the top of your fist between your thumb and first finger. This will form a ball shape. Use a spoon in your other hand to scoop this perfect ball shape off your fist and drop it into the hot water. The water helps to firm up the edges of the fish ball. Repeat until all the mixture has been used. It will make roughly 40 fish balls.

To cook the fish balls, add 1 tablespoon of salt to about 1 litre (34 fl oz/4¼ cups) of water in a large saucepan and bring to the boil. Lower the heat to a simmer, then slowly drop in each fish ball (be careful as they are really fragile before cooking). Boil for about 2–3 minutes, then scoop out the fish balls with a slotted spoon or spider. Make sure you don't overcrowd the pot with fish balls and cook them in batches.

To make the soup, you can use the water from cooking the fish balls if you want extra flavour (just remember to skim off any scum floating on the surface). Top this up with more water to make 1.5 litres (50 fl oz/6¼ cups) in a large cooking pot, then add the ginger, spring onions, chicken stock powder, sesame oil and pepper. Allow to boil for 15 minutes until you have a very tasty broth.

Now blanch the rehydrated noodles by pouring boiling water over them and allow to drain. Divide the noodles between bowls.

Add the fish balls (I like about six per person) to the broth in the cooking pot and bring to the boil. Once the fish balls start to float, cook for a couple of minutes, scoop them out and put on top of the noodles. Then ladle some of the broth over the fish balls and noodles before serving with blanched greens of your choice or a condiment such as chilli oil or soy sauce.

King Prawn Eggs

SERVES: 4
PREP: 10 minutes
COOK: 10 minutes

King prawns (shrimp) are considered an expensive food, but they can be stretched with other ingredients. This is a classic Cantonese dish that is super quick and simple to make – the eggs are also really fluffy and light.

INGREDIENTS

eggs	6
vegetable oil, for frying	
chicken stock powder	½ teaspoon
sugar	¼ teaspoon
cornflour (cornstarch) paste (page 17)	1 tablespoon
spring onion (scallion), chopped into 1 cm (½ in) pieces	1
raw king prawns (shrimp), shelled, deveined and butterflied down the middle (so they fan out when cooked)	200 g (7 oz)

COATING

salt	¼ teaspoon
white pepper	¼ teaspoon
cornflour (cornstarch)	1 teaspoon

METHOD

Beat the eggs in a bowl with a teaspoon of vegetable oil, the chicken stock powder, sugar and cornflour paste until light and airy (you will see bubbles on the surface). Then add the chopped spring onion and mix. Pat the prawns dry with some paper towels.

To make the coating, mix the salt and pepper in a bowl, then blend in the cornflour. Add the prawns to the bowl and coat thoroughly with the coating.

Heat a dry wok or large frying pan for about a minute, then add a tablespoon of vegetable oil and swirl to ensure you cover the wok/pan surface.

Fry off the prawns and keep tossing until they are pink in colour. This should only take about 30 seconds – you do not want them fully cooked. Remove the prawns and mix them in the beaten egg mixture.

Add another tablespoon of vegetable oil to the wok/pan over a high heat, then pour in the egg and prawn mixture. It should bubble rapidly around the edges. Cook for about 30 seconds, then use a fish slice to scoop the mixture off the bottom of the wok/pan and fold it on top of itself. This will allow the uncooked egg to fill the bottom of the wok/pan again.

Repeat the 30-second cooking process twice, then turn off the heat. Keep folding the egg on top of itself, using the residual heat until it is cooked through. If the egg mixture needs further cooking, return to a high heat and cook without folding (if the mixture starts to burn, then fold over again). You are now ready to serve.

TOP TIPS

- The longer you cook the egg mixture, the less fluffy it will be. So *do not* be tempted to push the egg back and forth in the pan/wok – you are not looking for Western-style scrambled eggs, but a fluffy, folded egg mixture.

- The cornflour paste in the marinade is the key ingredient as it keeps the moisture locked in the eggs and stops them drying out as quickly.

Scallops with Mushrooms and Pak Choi

SERVES: 4
PREP: 15 minutes
COOK: 25 minutes

This dish is traditionally made with abalone, but they are a delicacy and can be expensive, so I have modified the recipe by using scallops instead, which also speeds up the cooking time.

INGREDIENTS

small dried shiitake mushrooms	20
vegetable oil, for frying	
fresh ginger root, grated	15 g (½ oz)
garlic, grated	1 large clove
scallops	500 g (1 lb 2 oz)

SAUCE

oyster sauce	5 tablespoons
Shaoxing wine (or dry sherry or white wine)	1 tablespoon
chicken stock powder	1 teaspoon
sugar	¼ teaspoon
water or mushroom water	500 ml (17 fl oz/ generous 2 cups)
cornflour (cornstarch) paste (page 17)	1–2 tablespoons
salt and white pepper	

PAK CHOI

pak choi (bok choi), trimmed, leaves separated and core sliced into 4	250 g (9 oz), (approx. 2 heads)
salt (for boiling water)	1 teaspoon

TOP TIPS

- To cook this dish with fresh abalone, tenderise them first by bashing with a mallet and cooking this dish for about 1 hour.

- The dried shiitake mushrooms are used in many dishes throughout the book and using the water the mushrooms have been soaked in will make the dish more flavoursome.

METHOD

Rehydrate the shiitake mushrooms in 500 ml (17 fl oz/generous 2 cups) boiling water for a minimum of 20 minutes (keep the mushroom water).

Heat 2 tablespoons of vegetable oil in a wok or large frying pan over a high heat, then fry off the ginger and garlic, adding a splash of water to stop them burning. Allow the aromatics to be released from the fresh spices (about 30–60 seconds).

Next add the rehydrated mushrooms to the wok/pan and fry off for another couple of minutes.

Add the oyster sauce, Shaoxing wine, chicken stock powder, sugar and a pinch each of salt and pepper to the wok/pan. Taste and adjust the seasoning.

Pour in 500 ml (17 fl oz/generous 2 cups) of water (or use the reserved mushroom water and top up with more water if necessary). Then let everything bubble away for a further 15 minutes on a low simmering heat.

To cook the pak choi, half-fill a large cooking pot with water, add the teaspoon of salt and bring to the boil. Add the pak choi and blanch for 2–3 minutes. Cook to your taste: the longer you cook the pak choi, the softer it will become. Remove from the boiling water immediately and drain.

Pat the scallops dry with some paper towels, then add to the mushroom sauce and stir through, coating them thoroughly. Allow to simmer for a further 5 minutes until the scallops are just cooked but not overcooked. If the sauce is quite watery, add a tablespoon of cornflour paste at a time and bring to the boil to thicken. You are looking for a sauce that just coats the scallops.

Arrange the pak choi around the edge of a serving plate. Then pour the scallop mixture into the middle of the plate and serve with some hot, steaming basmati rice or as part of a large banquet.

Curry Fish Balls and Daikon Stew

SERVES: 4
PREP: 10 minutes
COOK: 30 minutes

Curried fish balls are a street market classic in Hong Kong, and you can buy skewers of curried fish balls in the market that are eaten out of a brown paper bag. The version I am showing you here is more of a dim sum classic because it includes daikon (mooli). There would usually be pig skin in this dish (I know this may seem foreign, but it is delicious and adds a fabulous texture). I also recently discovered that my little cousin Samantha loves this dish – she is only five years younger than me, but in my eyes she is still seven years old!

INGREDIENTS

fresh or frozen fish balls (see Fish Ball Noodle Soup, page 26, if you wish to make your own)	200 g (7 oz)

DAIKON

daikon (mooli), peeled and chopped into large, bite-size pieces	500 g (1 lb 2 oz)
brown sugar (for the boiling water)	1 heaped teaspoon

SAUCE

vegetable oil, for frying	
small onion, finely diced	1
garlic, finely chopped	2 large cloves
fresh ginger root, peeled and finely chopped	15 g (½ oz)
curry powder	2 tablespoons
hoisin sauce	1 tablespoon
oyster sauce	1 tablespoon
brown sugar	1 tablespoon
cornflour (cornstarch) paste (page 17)	1–2 tablespoons
salt and white pepper	

METHOD

To cook the daikon, pour approximately 750 ml (25 fl oz/3 cups) of water into a large cooking pot with the brown sugar and bring to the boil.

Add the pieces of daikon to the boiling liquid. Bring back to the boil, then boil for 5 minutes. Scoop out the pieces with a spider or slotted spoon. Keep the daikon water.

To make the sauce, heat 2 tablespoons of vegetable oil in a wok or large frying pan, then fry off the onion, garlic and ginger over a low heat until the onion softens. If it starts to burn, add a splash of water. This will take about 5 minutes.

Add another tablespoon of vegetable oil to the wok/pan along with the curry powder and fry for about 1–2 minutes until it becomes fragrant (add a splash of water if the curry powder starts to burn). Now add the hoisin sauce, oyster sauce and brown sugar and cook for another 2–3 minutes.

Return the daikon to the wok/pan, then add the fish balls and toss them in the curry sauce. Allow to cook and soak up the curry flavours for a couple of minutes.

Pour approximately 500 ml (17 fl oz/generous 2 cups) of the daikon water into the wok/pan to just cover the fish balls and daikon. Allow to simmer for 10 minutes until the daikon is cooked. If you would like the daikon very soft, then simmer for a further 5 minutes or so.

Check the consistency of the sauce. If you would like it thicker, add a tablespoon of cornflour paste at a time and bring to the boil. Season to taste with salt and pepper.

Serve the fish balls and daikon with some rice or noodles, or just on their own!

TOP TIP

- You can freeze this dish and then reheat again until piping hot. Remember to defrost thoroughly first.

POULTRY

02 二

家禽

Back in the olden days, it was customary in China to give gifts of live poultry for luck because having fowl was deemed a luxury, but times have changed. Chicken is usually served whole with the head, wings and feet intact for Chinese New Year and symbolises family unity. In Mandarin Chinese, 'chicken' ('ji' / 吉) is a homophone for 'lucky'.

CHAPTER TWO

THE MENU

COCA COLA
CHICKEN WINGS
36

MUM'S CRUNCHY
SESAME SEED
CHICKEN
38

CHINESE CHICKEN
AND POTATO STEW
41

CHICKEN, SWEETCORN
AND CARROT
42

SALTED CHILLI
CHICKEN
44

THE MENU

SALTED
CHICKEN EGGS
46

CHICKEN AND
CHESTNUTS
49

KUNG PO CHICKEN
50

WHITE CUT
CHICKEN
52

Coca Cola Wings

SERVES: 4
PREP: 10 minutes
COOK: 20 minutes

Coca cola was introduced to Hong Kong in the 1960s and has made its way into a couple of recipes – boiled cola with ginger and coca cola chicken. Coca cola wings are one of those dishes I remember Mum making and thinking: how are we allowed to eat these as she wouldn't let us drink a tin of coke when we were younger! I started making these wings for my kids only recently and they are gobbled up before they even eat their rice.

INGREDIENTS

CHICKEN WINGS

chicken wings, separated into wingettes and drummets	1 kg (2 lb 4 oz)
vegetable oil, for frying	
salt and white pepper	

SAUCE

fresh ginger root, peeled and sliced	30 g (1 oz)
Shaoxing wine	2 tablespoons
dark soy sauce	2 tablespoons
light soy sauce	1 tablespoon
garlic cloves, sliced	3
full-sugar cola	1 tin, (330 ml/ 11¼ fl oz/1⅓ cups)

METHOD

Put the wingettes and drummets in a saucepan, cover with cold water and bring to the boil. Then boil for 5 minutes, skimming off the impurities or scum that float on the surface with a large spoon. Use a slotted spoon to remove the wings and keep the chicken broth for other uses.

To make the sauce, heat 1 tablespoon of vegetable oil in a wok or large frying, add the ginger and garlic, then fry for about 30 seconds to start releasing the aromas. Then throw in the chicken wings and brown for about 3–5 minutes to add extra flavour.

Now add all the remaining sauce ingredients to the wok/pan. Bring to the boil, then lower to a simmer and cover with a lid. Allow to bubble away for about 15 minutes until the liquid has reduced to a sticky sauce.

Toss the wings in the sticky sauce, then season to taste with salt and pepper. Bring the heat up to full again, so the sauce caramelises and coats the lovely wings.

TOP TIPS

- For this recipe, you must use full-sugar cola as it is the caramelisation of the sugars that produces the thick sticky sauce. You can also use a zero or diet version of coke, but please note that the sauce will not thicken up, so add some cornflour (cornstarch) paste (page 17) and boil until thickened.

- Any leftover cooked little wings freeze well and can be kept for a month in the freezer.

- Use the chicken broth water to enhance the stock for the Crispy Chilli Egg Noodle Bowl (page 92).

Mum's Crunchy Sesame Seed Chicken

SERVES: 4
PREP: 15 minutes
COOK: 20 minutes

Mum experimented in the kitchen a lot, and this was one of the ideas she trialled on our takeaway menu. When we had fresh chicken breasts Mum used to make us separate out the mini fillet from the main breast. She always dabbled with ingredients that we already had in the takeaway. I guess that is why I love 'rustling up' dishes! The dip uses mayonnaise and ketchup because we sold 'burgers' from our 'Western' menu in the shop, so she made a simple Marie rose sauce for them.

INGREDIENTS

SESAME CHICKEN

mini chicken fillets	400 g (14 oz)
large egg, beaten	1
sesame seeds (black, white or a mixture)	100 g (3½ oz/ ⅔ cup)
vegetable oil, for frying	

MARINADE

sesame oil	1 teaspoon
light soy sauce	1 teaspoon
garlic powder (granules)	1 teaspoon
cornflour (cornstarch)	1 tablespoon
ground ginger	1 teaspoon
white pepper	¼ teaspoon
salt	¼ teaspoon

DIPPING SAUCE

mayonnaise	4 tablespoons
ketchup	4 tablespoons

METHOD

Marinade the chicken mini fillets in a bowl with all the marinade ingredients. Allow the chicken to marinate for 15 minutes.

Pour the beaten egg into the bowl of marinating chicken and mix in well. Sprinkle the sesame seeds onto a large plate.

Take each chicken piece, coat in the sesame seeds and then flip around in the seeds to ensure all sides are covered.

Heat 3 tablespoons of vegetable oil in a wok or large frying pan over a high heat, then lower to medium. Place about four pieces of chicken in the wok/pan at a time, ensuring they are not overcrowded, and allow to become golden on one side (about 3–4 minutes). Use a pair of tongs to flip over the chicken pieces and repeat for the other side.

Remove the chicken pieces from the wok/pan and transfer to some paper towels to remove excess oil. Repeat for the rest of the chicken pieces (you may need to add more oil to the wok/pan to prevent them sticking).

To serve, mix the dipping sauce ingredients in a bowl, then eat as a snack or with other dishes as part of a meal.

TOP TIPS

- When you have encrusted the chicken pieces with sesame seeds, you can also cook them in an air fryer at 180°C (350°F) for 10 minutes.

- The sesame chicken pieces can be frozen and cooked from frozen in a preheated oven or air fryer until piping hot.

Chinese Chicken and Potato Stew

SERVES: 4
PREP: 15 minutes
COOK: 40 minutes

This is pure comfort food in a bowl and served with hot basmati rice; it is very moreish. My Mum would make a huge pot of this stew and 'hoped' it would last until the next day for leftovers. I remember it didn't sometimes – I used to swim every day for my local club and I was a very hungry teenager!

INGREDIENTS

vegetable oil, for frying	
chicken drumsticks	500 g (1 lb 2 oz)
white potatoes, ideally Maris Piper, peeled and chopped into large chunks	4 (approx. 700 g/ 1 lb 9 oz)
garlic cloves, peeled and smashed	4
fresh ginger root, peeled and finely sliced	30 g (1 oz)
large spring onions (scallions), whites, chopped into 5 cm (2 in) lengths, and green tops, thinly sliced (keep both the white stalks and green tops)	2
chicken stock powder	1 teaspoon
dash of light soy sauce (optional)	
salt and white pepper	

SAUCE

light soy sauce	½ tablespoon
dark soy sauce	½ tablespoon
sesame oil	1 teaspoon
oyster sauce	1 tablespoon
sugar	1 teaspoon
Shaoxing wine	1 tablespoon
cornflour (cornstarch)	1 heaped teaspoon

TOP TIP

- This dish tastes even better the day after it is made, and so I like to make a larger batch of this and enjoy the leftovers the next day.

METHOD

Heat 2 tablespoons of vegetable oil in a wok or large frying pan over a high heat and brown the chicken drumsticks on all sides. Then set aside.

Mix all the sauce ingredients together in a bowl.

Pat the potato chunks dry with some paper towel. Heat 3 tablespoons of vegetable oil in the wok/pan and fry off the potato chunks until they are browned. This stops them turning into mashed potato when they are cooked later, but also provides extra flavour. You may need to fry the potato in batches and use more oil. Remove the potatoes and set aside.

Heat 2 tablespoons of vegetable oil in a large cooking pot over a high heat and fry off the garlic, ginger and the white stalks of the spring onions until fragrant (about 3–5 minutes).

Add the browned drumsticks to the pot followed by the sauce. Coat the drumsticks thoroughly and allow the sauce to reduce for about 2 minutes.

Sprinkle the chicken stock powder over the browned drumsticks and add the fried potatoes to the pot.

Add 500 ml (17 fl oz/generous 2 cups) of water to the pot, so it just covers the meat and potatoes (you may need more water depending on the size of your pot). Put the lid on the pot and allow everything to simmer for 15 minutes. Do not be tempted to add too much water, otherwise the potato will fall apart and become mash. Stir the pot occasionally to check the potato is not burning and sticking to the pot. Check the potatoes are ready – they may need another 10–15 minutes to soften.

Once the potatoes are cooked, season to taste with salt and pepper, but also add a dash of light soy sauce to give the dish a further umami taste. Finally, add the chopped green spring onion.

We always served this stew with basmati rice and as one of many dishes for dinner. Enjoy!

Chicken, Sweetcorn and Carrot

SERVES: 4
PREP: 10 minutes
COOK: 15 minutes

My big sister, Angela, flew across the world from Hong Kong to help me when baby Zander was only three weeks old. Angela made a big pot of this dish, so I could have it for a couple of days. This is a real family/child-friendly dish, as everything is diced up small and easily mixed with a hot bowl of steamed basmati rice. It is just delicious, and I have so many happy memories of this dish. Firstly, not having to cook for myself and, secondly, also knowing I was eating healthily, and it was all in one bowl. I have modified this dish to incorporate courgette (zucchini) to add even more vegetables for my children, and they love it.

INGREDIENTS

vegetable oil	1 tablespoon
chicken thighs and/or breast, cut into small dice	500 g (1 lb 2 oz)
large onion, diced	1
carrots, peeled and diced	2 (approx. 350 g/12 oz)
corn on the cob, kernels removed with a sharp knife	2 (approx. 250 g/9 oz)
courgette (zucchini), diced	1

MARINADE

cornflour (cornstarch)	2 teaspoons
light soy sauce	2 tablespoons
sesame oil	1 teaspoon

SAUCE

chicken stock	300 ml (10 fl oz/ 1¼ cups)
oyster sauce	2 tablespoons
cornflour (cornstarch) paste (page 17)	1–2 tablespoons (optional)
salt and white pepper	

METHOD

Make the marinade by mixing all the ingredients in a large bowl, then marinate the chicken for at least 10 minutes.

Heat the vegetable oil in a wok or large frying pan to a high heat and fry off the diced chicken until golden brown (about 5 minutes). Use a wooden spoon to keep tossing the pieces around.

Add the onion to the wok/pan and fry for a couple of minutes, then add the carrot and sweetcorn and fry for another couple of minutes. Finally, add the courgette and toss through all the other ingredients.

To make the sauce, pour the stock into the wok/pan along with the oyster sauce and allow to bubble away for a further 5 minutes or so. If you like your vegetables really soft, cook for a further 5 minutes or more. I like mine with a bit of a bite.

The cornflour used in the chicken marinade will help to thicken the sauce. If you do not think the sauce is thick enough, add a tablespoon of cornflour paste at a time, bring the dish to the boil and it will thicken. If you want more sauce, add more water/stock and thicken with cornflour paste. Taste and season with salt and pepper accordingly.

Serve with some rice or noodles.

TOP TIP

- Chop each ingredient to roughly the same size before you cook (apart from the sweetcorn), so everything cooks quickly.

Salted Chilli Chicken

SERVES: 4
PREP: 25 minutes
COOK: 25 minutes

INGREDIENTS

chicken breasts, finely sliced	4
vegetable oil, for frying	
spring onions (scallions), sliced, to garnish	
salt and white pepper	

MARINADE

cornflour (cornstarch)	2 teaspoons
salt	¼ teaspoon
white pepper	¼ teaspoon
light soy sauce	2 tablespoons
sesame oil	2 teaspoons

BATTER COATING

plain (all-purpose) flour	75 g (2½ oz/ generous ½ cup)
cornflour (cornstarch)	100 g (3½ oz/ ¾ cup)
pinch of salt and white pepper	
eggs, beaten (keep separate)	2

VEGETABLES

onion, sliced	1
sweet (bell) pepper, sliced (I prefer green pepper for colour contrast and taste)	1
garlic cloves, finely chopped	2 large cloves
finely chopped fresh ginger root	2 tablespoons
fresh red or green chilli, finely sliced	1 (or as much or as little as you want)

SALT AND CHILLI SPICE MIX

five-spice powder	1 teaspoon
salt	½ tablespoon
white pepper	½ teaspoon
sugar	½ tablespoon
dried red chilli (hot pepper) flakes	¼ teaspoon

METHOD

Preheat the oven to 180°C fan (400°F).

Mix all the ingredients for the marinade in a large bowl and marinate the chicken strips in advance – at least 10 minutes before cooking or up to the day before.

To make the batter coating, mix the plain flour, cornflour, salt and pepper together on a plate. Then dip the chicken strips first in the beaten egg, then in the flour mixture.

Heat about 1 cm (½ in) of vegetable oil in the bottom of a heavy-bottomed pot to a high temperature. Test the oil by dropping in a little bit of the batter to check the temperature – it should sizzle straightaway.

When frying the chicken strips, try to shake off any excess flour first. Fry the strips in batches and don't overcrowd the pot – they will only take about 1–2 minutes to cook on each side. Also, it is important not to overcook the chicken. Put the strips on a grill tray and transfer to the preheated oven, so they stay crisp.

Heat a little vegetable oil in a wok or large frying pan, add the onions and cook for a couple of minutes before adding the pepper. Next, add the garlic and ginger, then the chilli. Cook for a couple of minutes until the ginger and garlic become aromatic and fragrant.

Combine all the ingredients for the salt and chilli spice mix in a bowl, then mix half of this through the vegetables in the wok/pan.

Quickly add the chicken strips to the wok/pan and toss everything together until coated in the salt and chilli mix. Taste and add more mix if necessary – I sometimes use all the mix or add it to my rice or noodles to give them extra flavour!

Garnish the chicken with the spring onion and serve with rice. And enjoy!

TOP TIPS

- After cooking the chicken strips, tip the hot oil into a bowl, then once it is cold, strain through some paper towel to remove any bits and reuse another time.

- You can cheat and cook the chicken strips in an air fryer without frying them in oil. Just spray them with a little oil and cook at 180°C (350°F) for 10 minutes.

- Other meats, such as pork, beef or prawns (shrimp), can also be used for this dish.

Salted Chicken Eggs

MAKES: 10
PREP: 1 hour 15 minutes
BRINING TIME: 10–14 days

Growing up, these eggs were used to stretch out meals, but I also loved them in congee, a bowl of hot steaming rice porridge (see my Quick Congee recipe, page 91). The salted yolk is used for special recipes, such as moon cakes, zongzi (rice dumplings) and pastries. Traditionally, they would be made with duck eggs. They were supposedly developed in the 5th century to prolong the shelf life of duck eggs. They were believed to be highly nutritious and were brined for a month. I used chicken eggs for this recipe, as they are more readily available, and a vinegar mixture to speed up the brining process.

INGREDIENTS

large chicken eggs	10

BRINE

fine sea salt	125 g (4½ oz/½ cup)
water	700 ml (24 fl oz/ scant 3 cups)

EGG SOAK

distilled clear vinegar (the cheap and cheerful stuff)	200 ml (7 fl oz/ scant 1 cup)
cooled boiled water	600 ml (20 fl oz/2½ cups)

EGG RINSE

clear 40% proof alcohol (such as gin or vodka)	50 ml (1¾ fl oz/ 3½ tablespoons)

TOP TIPS

- Use the salted egg yolk for the delicious dim sum recipe, *Lava Custard Buns* on page 140.
- To keep the eggs for even longer, hard boil them, then cool and keep in the freezer for up to three months.

METHOD

Sterilise a large, heatproof glass jar with a lid large enough to hold 10 eggs. To do this, wash the jar well and put in a cooking pot along with the lid. Cover with water until submerged, then bring the water to a boil and boil for 2–3 minutes. You can also put the rubber seal in the boiling water if you are using a Kilner jar. Remove the jar and lid when the water has cooled a little and turn upside down onto some paper towel. The heat of the glass should evaporate the water.

To make the brine solution, add the sea salt and water to a large saucepan and bring to the boil. Once all the salt has dissolved, remove the pan from the heat. Leave to cool down to room temperature.

To make the egg soak, mix the vinegar and cooled boiled water in a bowl, then add the eggs gently, ensuring they are fully submerged in the vinegar mixture. You may need to use a smaller bowl to submerge all the eggs. Leave the eggs for 1 hour.

Carefully remove the eggs from the vinegar solution. You will notice that they will feel furry because a layer of shell has been dissolved by the acidic egg soak. Using your fingers, carefully rub off this furry layer and rinse it away under the tap. Be careful, as the eggs are now more fragile.

Pat the eggs dry with some paper towels and pour your choice of alcohol for the egg rinse into a small bowl. Roll each of the just-dried eggs in the alcohol to kill any bacteria on the surface.

Place each egg carefully in the sterilised jar, then pour the cooled brine on top of all the eggs. The eggs will start to float, so use a piece of crumpled baking parchment on top of the eggs and brine to push them all down and keep them submerged. Put the jar in a cool, dark cupboard.

Now you need to wait. I always put a reminder on my phone to check on the eggs. They will take 10 days to get the initial salty egg taste. Fourteen days is the maximum time to leave the eggs, otherwise they will be too salty.

To test the eggs on day 10, bring a cooking pot of water to the boil, then simmer one of the eggs for 10 minutes. Use a sharp knife to cut the egg in half, then taste the white and yolk to judge the saltiness. If you want the eggs to be saltier, leave the other eggs in the brine for a maximum of a further four days. Do not waste the test egg – enjoy it by chopping it up into a bowl of rice and some steamed veggies.

Once you are happy with the eggs, remove from the jar, dry gently and wrap each one in cling film (plastic wrap). The eggs will keep in the fridge for two weeks, or you can boil them so they keep for a month in the fridge in an airtight container.

Chicken and Chestnuts

SERVES: 4
PREP: 20 minutes
COOK: 30 minutes

This is my quick version of the dish, but it still packs in the flavour. Chicken wings are delicious and chicken thighs are super tender however you cook them, but for time and speed chicken mini fillets have been used in this recipe. This dish is sort of made in reverse to get the most out of the sauce flavours first.

INGREDIENTS

dried wood ear mushroom	15 g (½ oz)
chicken mini fillets	400 g (14 oz)
vegetable oil, for frying	
Shaoxing wine	2 tablespoons
dark soy sauce	1 tablespoon
salt	¼ teaspoon
soft brown sugar	1 tablespoon
sesame oil	1 teaspoon
cooked whole chestnuts	1 packet (approx. 180–200 g /6½–7 oz)
cornflour (cornstarch) paste (page 17)	1–2 tablespoons
salt and white pepper	

MARINADE

dark soy sauce	1 tablespoon
sesame oil	1 teaspoon
cornflour (cornstarch)	1 teaspoon

AROMATICS

star anise	1
spring onions (scallions), cut into 5 cm (2 in) pieces	4
garlic, sliced	1 large garlic clove
fresh ginger root, peeled and sliced	15 g (½ oz)

METHOD

If the wood ear mushroom are very large in size then slice into strips. Rehydrate the wood ear mushroom in 250 ml (8 fl oz/1 cup) of boiling water and keep the water.

Mix all the ingredients for the marinade in a bowl, then marinate the chicken for at least 15 minutes.

Heat 2 tablespoons of vegetable oil in a wok or large frying pan and seal the chicken first (about 3–4 minutes for each side). Cook the chicken in batches and avoid overcrowding the wok/pan. Set the chicken aside once cooked and do not clean the wok/pan.

Add another tablespoon of vegetable oil to the wok/pan and slowly fry off the aromatics – the star anise, spring onion, garlic and ginger – over a low/medium heat for about 5 minutes until you can smell the aromas.

Then deglaze the wok/pan over a high heat, adding the Shaoxing wine followed by the dark soy sauce, salt, brown sugar and sesame oil, and stir.

Add the chestnuts and rehydrated wood ear mushroom to the wok/pan and mix everything together. Pour in about 100 ml (3½ fl oz/scant ½ cup) of the wood ear mushroom soaking water and simmer for 5 minutes with the lid on. If you would like more sauce, then add more liquid or some stock.

Finally, return the chicken to the wok/pan and simmer for a further 5 minutes with the lid on. Season to taste with salt and pepper.

Check the consistency of the sauce: if it is not thick enough (the chestnuts will help thicken the sauce when they break down a bit in cooking), add a tablespoon of cornflour paste at a time and bring to the boil.

This dish delivers on taste and textures, and I absolutely love it served with some rice.

TOP TIP

- This can be a slow-cooked dish. If slow cooking, I recommend using chicken wingettes instead of the mini fillets. Simply replace like for like and follow the same steps, but allow the dish to simmer for at least 15–20 minutes to ensure the wings are cooked through. The wings add extra flavour, but the meat does not become tough when cooked for a longer period.

Kung Po Chicken

SERVES: 4
PREP: 20 minutes
COOK: 20 minutes

Kung po chicken is my husband's absolute favourite Chinese takeaway dish, so here it is, my simplified version. My husband loves it because he describes it as a 'jacked-up' version of a sweet and sour.

INGREDIENTS

chicken breasts	400 g (14 oz)
vegetable oil, for frying	
cornflour (cornstarch) paste (page 17)	2–3 tablespoons
large handful of toasted cashew nuts, to garnish	
salt and white pepper	

MARINADE

light soy sauce	2 teaspoons
cornflour (cornstarch)	1 tablespoon

SAUCE

finely chopped garlic	1 tablespoon
ketchup	8 tablespoons
hoisin sauce	8 tablespoons
brown sugar	1 tablespoon
rice wine vinegar	1 tablespoon
five-spice powder	1 teaspoon
dried chilli (hot pepper) flakes	¼ tablespoon

VEGETABLES

vegetable oil	1 tablespoon
onion, cut into large dice	1
carrot, peeled and sliced	1
green (bell) pepper, deseeded and cut into chunks	1
water chestnuts	1 small tin (227 g/8 oz)
bamboo shoots	1 small tin (227 g/8 oz)

METHOD

Finely slice the chicken across the width of the breasts, so you have oval pieces about 5 mm (¼ in) thick.

To make the marinade, mix the soy sauce and cornflour in a bowl, then marinate the chicken for approximately 15 minutes.

To make the sauce, heat 1 teaspoon of vegetable oil in a small cooking pot and fry off the garlic for about 1 minute until fragrant.

Add the remaining sauce ingredients to the pot and allow to simmer for about 2–3 minutes. Add a splash of water if the mixture starts to burn or stick to the pot to loosen the sauce. The longer the sauce bubbles away, the stickier and more caramelised it will become.

Heat 2 tablespoons of oil in a wok or large frying pan and fry off the chicken in batches – you want the chicken to be slightly golden brown, which will take about 5 minutes per batch. Remove the chicken from the wok/pan and set aside. Do not clean the wok.

To cook the vegetables, add 1 tablespoon of oil to the same wok/pan and fry off the onion, carrot and pepper with a splash of water, so they do not burn (about 2 minutes). You want the onion to be slightly golden. Then add the water chestnuts and bamboo shoots.

Add the chicken to the vegetables in the wok/pan and then the sauce. Allow to bubble away for about 5 minutes. The sauce will become thinner due to the liquid released from the vegetables. If you want the sauce to thicken, add a tablespoon of cornflour paste at a time and bring to the boil. Season to taste with salt and pepper.

Toast the cashew nuts in a dry frying pan, ensuring they do not burn. Then top the dish with the cashew nuts when you are ready to serve.

This dish is delicious served with some rice or chow mein.

TOP TIPS

- If you want a spicier sauce, add more chilli flakes, and if you want it sharper, add more rice wine vinegar.

- The sauce freezes well, so you can double the batch and freeze it for up to a month. It also keeps well in the fridge for over a week.

- If you do not have a green (bell) pepper any other colour would do, the green pepper gives it a good contrast in taste.

White Cut Chicken

SERVES: 4
PREP: 10 minutes
COOK: 1 hour

A whole chicken symbolises happiness, prosperity and family togetherness. It is therefore not to be left off a Chinese New Year menu. This is a variation on the Hainanese chicken recipe from my *Simply Chinese* cookbook, but the chicken is steamed instead of poached. A very simple but tasty recipe!

INGREDIENTS

whole chicken	1 (approx. 1.3 kg/3 lb)
fine sea salt	2 teaspoons
sesame oil	2 tablespoons

CHICKEN CAVITY PASTE

garlic	1½ large garlic cloves
spring onions (scallions), finely sliced	40 g (1½ oz) (about 4)
fresh ginger root, peeled	40 g (1½ oz)
sea salt	1 tablespoon

GINGER AND SPRING ONION SAUCE

fresh ginger root, peeled and grated	15 g (½ oz)
spring onions (scallions), finely chopped	30 g (1 oz)
sea salt	½ teaspoon
vegetable oil	2 tablespoons

TOP TIPS

- If you do not have a large enough steamer, use a large soup pot with a lid. Fill the pot with a couple of inches of water, then place a small heatproof bowl upside down on the bottom. Then balance a large plate or bowl on top to steam the chicken.

- The liquid that collects in the dish the chicken is steamed in is delicious, so I sometimes use this as a base for a broth or stock, or even pour it over rice.

METHOD

To prepare the chicken, scrub the skin with 1 teaspoon of fine sea salt and add 1 teaspoon to the cavity. Rinse the chicken inside and out under the tap, being careful not to splash the water about too much (make sure you wash and sanitise your sink thoroughly afterwards).

To make the cavity paste, place the garlic, spring onion and ginger on a cutting board and chop vigorously until you have a paste. Add the sea salt to the paste and then rub this mixture into the cavity of the chicken. This gives so much flavour to the chicken from the inside out. You can also use a mortar and pestle or a food processor to blitz the paste ingredients.

Bring some water in the cooking pot of a steamer to a boil, then place the chicken in a heatproof dish and lower into the steamer – be careful not to scald yourself here (I usually wear rubber gloves to do this).

Now steam the chicken with the lid on over a high heat for 25 minutes. Do not lift off the lid! Top up the steamer with more water if necessary. Lower to a medium heat. Steam for another 25 minutes, then turn off the heat. Leave the chicken in the steamer with the lid on and allow to cool for at least 10 minutes.

Lift the chicken from the steamer and drain any liquid that has collected in the cavity into the dish it was sitting in.

Brush the chicken with the sesame oil all over the skin. Chop the chicken into chunks when cooled and assemble on a large plate.

To make the ginger and spring onion sauce, mix the ginger, spring onion and salt in a small heatproof bowl (you can speed things up by blitzing the ginger in a food processor and then add the spring onion at the end).

Bring the 2 tablespoons of vegetable oil to smoking point in a small cooking pot. You will see the surface of the oil rippling when it reaches smoking point – test the temperature with the end of a wooden spoon. Immediately pour this boiling oil over the ginger and spring onion in the bowl.

Serve the steamed chicken with the ginger and spring onion sauce.

MEAT

03

三

肉
類

Eating meat demonstrated wealth in China. For feasts, when pork, beef and mutton were cooked in large quantities that were 'just enough' was not acceptable. Whole roast pigs were customary at large celebrations like weddings. The Chinese word character for 'pig' (豕) is found within the word character for 'family' (家). This is because pigs were kept indoors with their owners and therefore given a home – you can see there is a 'roof' in the character for family.

CHAPTER THREE

THE MENU

THE MENU

Pork Belly in Black Vinegar

SERVES: 4
PREP: 10 minutes
COOK: 1 hour

This recipe is based on a very traditional pork trotter, ginger and vinegar dish, which was made for confinement mothers because it was believed to provide nourishment and replenish energy. However, it required a lot of ingredients. So, I decided to showcase this pork belly and black vinegar recipe in a nod to the confinement dish. The pork belly is boiled first, then plunged into cold water and cooked again. This gives the pork a wonderful texture, reminiscent of the pork trotter dish. The flavours of the sweet and sour are there, but an extra layer of flavour is added by the garlic.

INGREDIENTS

PORK BELLY

pork belly, chopped into large, bite-size chunks	500 g (1 lb 2 oz)
vegetable oil, for frying	

SAUCE

fresh ginger root, peeled and sliced into rounds	30 g (1 oz)
garlic, finely sliced	1 large garlic clove
brown sugar	4 tablespoons
Shaoxing wine	1½ tablespoons
black vinegar	4 tablespoons
dark soy sauce	3 tablespoons
salt and white pepper	

METHOD

Bring about 1 litre (34 fl oz/4¼ cups) of water to the boil in a cooking pot, then add the pork belly pieces and bring up to the boil again for 10 minutes. This removes any gamey taste and renders some of the pork fat. Remove the pork with a slotted spoon and set aside.

Heat 1 tablespoon of vegetable oil in a wok or large frying pan over a high heat, then add the pork belly pieces and sear for about 5–8 minutes to give them some colour.

Push the pork belly pieces to one side of the wok/pan. Some fat should have been released from the pork (if not, add another tablespoon of oil).

To make the sauce, fry off the ginger and garlic in the wok/pan for about 1 minute.

Add the sugar, Shaoxing wine, black vinegar and soy sauce and approximately 250 ml (8 fl oz/1 cup) of water (it should just cover all the pieces of meat).

Pop the lid on the wok/pan and simmer for 30 minutes, then reduce the heat to low and leave the lid slightly ajar. Allow to cook for a further 15 minutes.

Taste one of the pork belly pieces at the 45-minute mark. If it is still chewy, cook for a further 10–15 minutes with the lid fully on. You want the pork to melt in your mouth and burst with flavour.

Adjust the seasoning to taste by adding more vinegar or sugar, or balance with some salt and pepper – trust your tastebuds!

TOP TIPS

- This dish freezes well and can be kept in the freezer for a month.

- If you do not have time, but love the taste of this dish, instead of boiling and browning the pork belly, finely slice some pork loin, fillet or shoulder and flash-fry for a couple of minutes. Then follow the next few steps without adding the pork, cooking the sauce for only 15 minutes and using just 125 ml (4 fl oz/½ cup) of water. Then toss in the flash-fried pork pieces and allow to reduce for another couple of minutes, so the sticky sauce coats the pieces of pork.

Traditional Char Siu Pork

SERVES: 6
PREP: The day before
COOK: 40 minutes

Char means 'fork' and *siu* means 'roast/ burn', which is how *char siu* used to be cooked – on a fork over a large, open flame. The main traditional ingredient is the red fermented bean curd, which gives the pork its red colouring (the colour comes from the fermentation of the red yeast rice used to make the curd). It also has a depth of flavour that can be imitated by using oyster sauce and extra Shaoxing wine. Pork is eaten at celebratory times such as Chinese New Year as it symbolises strength, wealth and blessings.

INGREDIENTS

PORK

pork shoulder (with some fat marbled through the meat)	1 kg (2 lb 4 oz)
honey, plus extra if needed	3 tablespoons
vegetable oil, for frying	

MARINADE

red fermented bean curd, mashed with 1 tablespoon of liquid from the jar	2–3 cubes
hoisin sauce	80 g (2¾ oz)
honey	40 g (1½ oz)
black treacle	30 g (1 oz)
dark soy sauce	30 g (1 oz)
five-spice powder	10 g (¼ oz)
garlic, finely chopped	about 1 large clove
oil	1 tablespoon
salt	¼ teaspoon
red food colouring (optional)	2 teaspoons

METHOD

Make the marinade the night before you plan to cook. Place a bowl on top of a set of digital scales and put a sandwich bag in the bowl. Then measure all the marinade ingredients directly into the bag.

Slice the pork shoulder lengthways into thin, uniform pieces about 2.5 cm (1 in) deep and 5–7.5 cm (2–3 in) wide.

Add the pork pieces to the bag and use your hands to massage the marinade into the meat. Place the bag flat on a baking tray, so the marinade covers all the meat, and keep in the fridge overnight.

The next day, when you are ready to cook, preheat the oven to 200°C fan (425°F).

Remove the marinated char siu pieces from the fridge and place on a grill tray lined with some tin foil to catch the drips.

Pour the leftover marinade in the bag into a bowl and mix with 3 tablespoons of honey, to give you a really sticky glaze.

Roast the char siu in the oven for 20 minutes, then remove and baste with the glaze. Grill the char siu pieces for approximately 5 minutes, then use tongs to flip the pieces over and baste with more glaze.

Continue basting and turning the pieces until all sides are sticky and the characteristic burned/ charred bits appear. It will take 10–20 minutes to get the desired result, but less time if you have smaller char siu pieces. You need a maximum of about 40 minutes for perfect char siu.

Once you are happy, brush the char siu with honey on all sides to make it glisten. Serve with rice or noodles, or add to countless other dishes to bulk them out.

TOP TIPS

- Any leftover char siu will freeze well and can be kept in the freezer for a month.
- You can use leftovers for the following recipes: Yung Chow Fried Rice (page 96), Traditional Spring Rolls (page 128) and Char Siu Puff (page 134).

Taro and Pork Belly

SERVES: 6
PREP: 30 minutes
COOK: 1 hour 30 minutes

This dish is a must at Chinese New Year and it is of Hakka origin. The Hakkas are a Han Chinese subgroup and originated in central China from Cantonese-speaking provinces. My Dad is of Hakka origin and my family settled in Hong Kong. Hakka is a dialect on its own – I have not mastered the language at all, but can understand a few phrases. If you cannot find any taro, you can use sweet potato instead. It is surprisingly tasty and easier to get hold of.

INGREDIENTS

taro or sweet potatoes	1 large (approx. 400 g/14 oz)
vegetable oil, for frying	
pork belly	500 g (1 lb 2 oz)
dark soy sauce	1 tablespoon
white spring onion (scallion) ends, finely sliced (retain the green tops)	25 g (1 oz)
fresh ginger root, peeled and finely chopped	10 g (¼ oz)
garlic, finely chopped	1½ large garlic cloves
cornflour (cornstarch) paste (page 17)	1–2 tablespoons
salt and white pepper	

SAUCE

red fermented bean curd, mashed with 1 tablespoon of liquid from the jar	2 cubes
light soy sauce	2 tablespoons
oyster sauce	1 tablespoon
brown sugar	2 tablespoons
hoisin sauce	1 tablespoon
Shaoxing wine	1 tablespoon
sesame oil	1 teaspoon
white pepper	¼ teaspoon
five-spice powder	1 teaspoon
chicken stock powder	1 teaspoon

METHOD

Peel the taro or sweet potato, chop into half-moons about 5 mm (¼ in) thick and shallow-fry in some vegetable oil until golden brown.

Put enough water in a saucepan to submerge the pork belly and boil for 10 minutes, skin side down, and then for a further 10 minutes, meat side down. Pat dry with some paper towels.

Heat 4 tablespoons of vegetable oil in a wok or large frying pan, fry the pork belly skin side down until browned (be careful as it will spit) and then flip and brown the underside.

Immediately place the pork belly in a bowl of cold tap water. The process of plunging the pork belly into cold water gives the meat a slightly chewy but yummy texture and makes it easier to cut.

Brush the underside of the pork belly with the dark soy sauce. Then cut on a chopping board into strips about 5 mm (¼ in) thick and 5 cm (2 in) long.

Arrange the pork belly pieces in a layer on the bottom of a heatproof dish that will fit a steamer, then add a layer of taro/sweet potato. Keep layering the pork and taro/sweet potato until they are used up.

Heat 1 tablespoon of vegetable oil in a saucepan and fry off the spring onion, ginger and garlic for about 1 minute until fragrant. Then add all the sauce ingredients and 250 ml (8 fl oz/1 cup) of water, and allow to simmer for a couple of minutes until bubbling.

Pour the sauce all over the meat and taro/sweet potato in the dish, then wrap tightly with tin foil and pop in a steamer for about 1 hour 15 minutes.

Remove the tin foil (be careful as it will be hot), then use a plate to hold the ingredients in the dish as you drain the liquid into the pan in which you made the sauce – it will be very watery. Taste the sauce and season accordingly.

Now, firmly press a large plate against the dish containing the pork belly and taro/sweet potato and flip so everything is out of the dish (it should hold its shape).

Bring the sauce in the saucepan to a boil, adding 1–2 tablespoons of cornflour paste at a time to thicken, then pour all over the pork belly.

Garnish with some of the green tops from the spring onions before serving.

TOP TIPS

- If you are short on time, the pork belly can be sliced into thinner than 5 mm (¼ in) pieces and will cook more quickly.

- This is another great dish that can be frozen if you have any leftovers.

Minced Beef and Egg Bowl

SERVES: 4
PREP: 10 minutes
COOK: 25 minutes

Growing up, we always had steaming hot basmati rice in the rice cookers in the takeaway, so Dad would crack an egg into a bowl of hot rice, drizzle over some soy sauce, mix everything up, and wolf it down! I asked him about this recently, and he said he used to eat the rice as a child when his parents were at work. He and his siblings were young and didn't know how to cook properly, so they would steam rice, crack an egg, add some soy sauce and also add a spoonful of pork dripping.

This recipe combines two dishes because I enjoy different textures and lots of flavour, plus I like to ensure all nutrient boxes are ticked in a meal. Using mince and peas together, as I have done here, is really traditional, while the raw cracked egg is cooked when it is mixed through the super-hot mince and rice and makes the dish so rich and creamy. I see this as a Chinese steak tartare crossed with a rice carbonara!

INGREDIENTS

vegetable oil, for frying	
minced (ground) beef	500 g (1 lb 2 oz)
onion, finely diced	1
Shaoxing wine	2 tablespoons
oyster sauce	3 tablespoons
dark soy sauce	1 teaspoon
light soy sauce	1 tablespoon
sesame oil	2 teaspoons
chicken stock powder	1 teaspoon
cornflour (cornstarch) paste (page 17)	3 tablespoons
fresh garden peas or frozen peas	150 g (5½ oz)
fresh raw eggs	4
salt and white pepper	

METHOD

Heat 1 teaspoon of vegetable oil in a wok or large frying pan and brown the minced beef for about 5 minutes.

Mix the onion with the mince, then add the Shaoxing wine and fry for a couple of minutes.

Next add the oyster sauce, dark soy sauce, light soy sauce, sesame oil, chicken stock powder and a pinch of white pepper, and allow to simmer for about 5 minutes.

Pour 500 ml (17 fl oz/generous 2 cups) of water into the wok/pan and bring to the boil, then simmer for a further 10 minutes.

Add the cornflour paste a tablespoon at a time and bring to the boil again. If you want the sauce to be thicker, add more cornflour paste.

Add the peas to the wok/pan and stir through. Season to taste with salt and pepper, if required.

Serve over a bowl of steaming basmati rice, top with a freshly cracked raw egg and mix through.

TOP TIPS

- For a vegetarian option, make with Quorn mince instead of beef mince.

- If you are not too keen on raw eggs, make four wells in the mince with the back of a large tablespoon 5 minutes after adding the water to the wok/pan and crack the eggs into the wells. Put a lid on the wok/pan (or make a makeshift one using foil), then cook for the remaining 5 minutes to allow the whites to cook through.

Crispy Peking Beef

SERVES: 4
PREP: 15 minutes
COOK: 25 minutes

Another takeaway classic, but using household condiments such as tomato purée and clear distilled vinegar. This is a very quick and easy recipe and ticks all the boxes for a takeaway craving.

INGREDIENTS

rump steak, fat removed	500 g (1 lb 2 oz)
vegetable oil, for frying	
spring onion (scallion), sliced, to garnish	

MARINADE

cornflour (cornstarch)	1 teaspoon
soy sauce	1 tablespoon
sesame oil	1 teaspoon
pinch of salt and white pepper	

BATTER COATING

eggs, beaten	2
plain (all-purpose) flour	8 tablespoons
cornflour (cornstarch)	8 tablespoons
pinch of salt and white pepper	

VEGETABLES

medium onion, sliced	1
large carrot, peeled and sliced	1
red (bell) pepper, deseeded and sliced	1

PEKING SAUCE

white sugar (granulated or caster/superfine)	6 tablespoons
clear distilled vinegar	6 tablespoons
tomato purée (paste)	5 tablespoons
water	8 tablespoons
hoisin sauce	6 tablespoons
five-spice powder	3 teaspoons
salt	½ teaspoon

METHOD

Cut the steak into strips (against the grain), then add to a bowl with all the marinade ingredients. You can marinate the steak 10 minutes prior to cooking or up until the day before. When you are ready to cook, preheat the oven to 180°C fan (400°F).

To make the batter coating, put the steak strips into a bowl with the beaten egg. In a separate bowl with the plain flour, cornflour, salt and pepper, dip the steak strips in to coat with the seasoned flour mixture.

Heat about 1 cm (½ in) of vegetable oil in the bottom of a heavy-duty cooking pot or deep-fat fryer over a high heat. Test the temperature of the oil by dropping in some of the batter – it should sizzle straightaway.

Fry the steak strips in batches, shaking off any excess flour before adding to the pot/fryer. Try not into overcrowd the pot/fryer, as the strips will only take about 1–2 minutes to cook on each side. Do not overcook the steak. Transfer the steak strips to a grill tray and keep in the preheated oven to stay crisp.

Add a little vegetable oil to a wok or large frying pan, then fry off the onion, carrot and pepper. Add 1 tablespoon of water to help soften the vegetables. Cook for a couple of minutes until the onion is softened but not burned.

Next add all the ingredients for the Peking sauce to the wok/pan – you will also need to add more water at this stage as the sauce will be very thick. I suggest about 4 tablespoons of cold water.

Let everything bubble away (you will start to smell the sauce caramelising). Bubble for another 3–4 minutes until you have a sticky sauce.

Add the steak strips to the wok/pan, then quickly toss so that everything is coated in the sauce. Cook for another 2 minutes, then garnish with the spring onion and serve with some rice.

TOP TIPS

- You can make this dish with any meat such as chicken, pork or prawns (shrimp), or even a meat alternative.

- Save time by prepping and freezing the crisped pieces of meat in advance or crisp it up in the oven just before you need it.

- Make the sauce in advance and freeze for up to 1 month or keep in the fridge for up to a week.

- After cooking the beef strips, tip the hot oil into a bowl, then once it is cold, strain through some paper towel to remove any bits and reuse another time.

Beef Mince and Choot Choi

SERVES: 4
PREP: 15 minutes
COOK: 20 minutes

Pickled snow cabbage (choot choi) was one of those ingredients my Mum always had – it was in terracotta and glass jars as well as tins. For this recipe, I am using the tinned variety. I did not realise until writing up this recipe that lots of vegetables are pickled and the one Mum used for the dishes I loved was pickled snow cabbage. I stood for about 30 minutes in the Chinese supermarket trying to locate it as there were so many varieties, but I finally found the brand my Mum used – Fuxing pickled cabbage!

METHOD

Heat 1 tablespoon of vegetable oil in a wok or large frying pan and fry the ginger and garlic for a couple of minutes until fragrant – make sure they do not burn.

Add the minced beef and cook for a further 2–3 minutes until the mince changes colour.

Add the remainder of the ingredients apart from the choot choi and water to the wok/pan and simmer for 2 minutes. Then add the pickled cabbage and water, and simmer for a further 5 minutes.

Season to taste with salt and pepper – this dish plays on your tastebuds, having a saltiness/umami flavour from the oyster sauce. Then it has the sharpness from the pickled cabbage. If you want to balance the flavour of the saltiness, add another pinch of sugar.

Serve with noodles, rice or steamed mantou buns (page 142).

INGREDIENTS

vegetable oil, for frying	
fresh ginger root, peeled and finely sliced	10 g (¼ oz)
garlic, finely sliced	1 large garlic clove
minced (ground) beef	500 g (1 lb 2 oz)
Shaoxing wine	1 tablespoon
oyster sauce	1 tablespoon
sugar	1 teaspoon
sesame oil	1 teaspoon
white pepper	½ teaspoon
cornflour (cornstarch) paste (page 17)	2 tablespoons
choot choi (pickled snow cabbage), drained and cut into bite-sized pieces	1 small tin (200 g/7 oz)
water	200 ml (7 fl oz/ scant 1 cup)
salt and white pepper	

TOP TIP

• You can also use this type of pickled snow cabbage in other soup noodle dishes (Shredded Chicken and Choot Choi Noodles, page 88), as my Mum did.

SOUP

04 四湯

Soup would take the place of water at our family dinners and we were only allowed to sip Mum's more nutritious soup if we were thirsty. Cantonese people believe that clear, broth-like soups alleviate various ailments, rejuvenating energy, boosting immunity and restoring yin and yang. Using meat bones in the soup stock was crucial, as this releases lots of vitamins, minerals and collagen and builds and strengthens cartilage, bone and skin. So use meat on the bone for that extra health kick!

CHAPTER FOUR

THE MENU

THE MENU

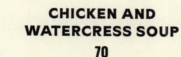

CHICKEN AND
WATERCRESS SOUP
70

PORK AND
LOTUS ROOT SOUP
72

ABC SOUP
75

SPINACH EGG
DROP SOUP
76

HOT POT
78

DRUNKEN
CHICKEN SOUP
80

Chicken and Watercress Soup

SERVES: 8–10
PREP: 10 minutes
COOK: 1 hour 15 minutes

Watercress soup is quite distinctive in flavour and Mum loved it, so we had to love it too! The watercress should be wild watercress, which you can find in Asian supermarkets. Otherwise, use store-bought watercress salad leaves, but add an additional 250 g (9 oz) for extra flavour. This soup is usually made with pork ribs, but I enjoy it with the mild sweetness of the chicken legs. I have also subbed in blanched almonds to add vitamin E, fibre and minerals. Traditionally, you would use bitter almonds, but I think ordinary blanched almonds are a really good substitute.

METHOD

Bring the water to a boil in a large soup pot, then add the chicken and boil for 20 minutes – skim off any scum from the surface to keep the soup clear.

Add the shiitake mushrooms, red dates, almonds, carrots, goji berries, chicken stock powder and 1 teaspoon of salt. Bring to the boil again, then boil for 10 minutes before reducing the heat and simmering with the lid on the pot until the carrots are soft (about 20 minutes).

Add the watercress and simmer for a further 25 minutes – the pot will look as if it is overflowing, but the watercress will wilt. Season to taste with salt and pepper.

INGREDIENTS

water	4 litres (8½ pints/4 quarts)
skinless chicken legs	4–6 skinless chicken legs, bones kept in
large dried shiitake mushrooms	4
dried red dates	60 g (2 oz) (about 8 large dates)
blanched almonds	50 g (1¾ oz/ ⅓ cup)
carrots, peeled and chopped into chunks	2 (approx. 200 g/7 oz)
dried goji berries	25 g (1 oz)
chicken stock powder (optional)	1 teaspoon
wild watercress, washed well and trimmed if the stalks are woody at the bottom	approx. 500 g (1 lb 2 oz)
salt and white pepper	

TOP TIP

- The soup tastes even better the next day and will keep for four days in the fridge. Always bring the soup to a roaring boil before serving to kill off any bacteria.

Pork and Lotus Root Soup

SERVES: 8–10
PREP: 10 minutes
COOK: 2 hours 15 minutes

Lotus root has an unusual, crunchy, starchy texture and is great in stir-fries, steamed, deep-fried and in soups. It is high in vitamins, minerals and fibre and therefore, as you could imagine, my Mum often made lotus root soup. Pork shoulder/butt or ribs can be used here – I chose shoulder to try something different and the flavour was still super good.

METHOD

Put the pork in a bowl and add the ginger, then pour over the 1 litre (34 fl oz/4½ cups) of boiling water to scald the meat. Leave to sit for 5 minutes, then remove the meat and ginger slices and pat dry with some paper towels.

Bring 3 litres (6 pints/3 quarts) of water to the boil in a large soup pot, then add the pork and ginger, lotus root, peanuts, red dates and chicken stock powder (if using). Once the liquid comes to the boil again, boil for 10 minutes.

Put the lid on the pot and simmer on low for 2 hours. Season to taste with salt and pepper.

INGREDIENTS

pork shoulder/butt	250 g (9 oz)
fresh ginger root, peeled and sliced	10 g (¼ oz)
boiling water	1 litre (34 fl oz/ 4¼ cups) + 3 litres (6 pints/ 3 quarts of water for soup
small lotus roots, peeled and cut into 1 cm (½ in) slices	2 (approx. 250 g/9 oz)
skinless peanuts	100 g (3½ oz/ ⅔ cup)
dried red dates	60 g (2 oz) (about 8 large dates)
chicken stock powder (optional)	1 teaspoon
salt and white pepper	

TOP TIPS

- The soup tastes even better the next day and will keep in the fridge for four days. Always bring the soup to a roaring boil before serving to kill off any bacteria.

- Finely slice any leftover lotus root to make Lotus Root Crisps (page 119).

- If you can only get hold of peanuts with their skins, pour boiling water over them and rub off the skin. You can also leave the skins on – this will just make the soup darker in colour.

ABC Soup

SERVES: 8–10
PREP: 10 minutes
COOK: 1 hour 15 minutes

Mum used to make this soup all the time, as it was quick and easy. The English translation of the dish is pork ribs, potato, carrot and tomato soup. I only recently discovered that it also had a different name: ABC soup. This is because it contains vitamin A (an antioxidant) from the tomatoes and carrots (in the beta-carotene form), which is essential for vision and the immune system; vitamin B from the pork, which is essential for the functioning of body/brain cells and tissues and helping the body convert food to energy; and vitamin C (an antioxidant) found in the tomatoes, sweetcorn and potatoes.

METHOD

Fill a large soup pot with the water and bring to the boil. Add the pork ribs to the pot and boil for 15 minutes, scooping off the scum from the surface. These are the impurities from the pork ribs.

Add the potatoes, tomatoes, carrots, onion, corn on the cob, 2 teaspoons of salt and chicken stock powder (if using) to the pot and put the lid on. Boil for 15 minutes and then simmer for a further 45 minutes. Season to taste with salt and pepper.

INGREDIENTS

water	4 litres (8½ pints/ 4 quarts)
pork ribs	approx. 500 g (1 lb 2 oz)
white potatoes (I use Maris Piper), peeled and chopped into large chunks	500 g (1 lb 2 oz)
tomatoes, quartered	400 g (14 oz)
carrots, peeled and cut into chunks	350 g (12 oz) (about 4 large carrots)
large onions, roughly chopped	2
fresh corn on the cob, chopped into four pieces each	2
chicken stock powder (optional)	1 teaspoon
salt and white pepper	

TOP TIP

- The soup tastes even better the next day and will keep in the fridge for four days. Always bring the soup to a roaring boil before serving to kill off any bacteria.

Spinach Egg Drop Soup

SERVES: 4
PREP: 10 minutes
COOK: 15 minutes

I took inspiration for this quick soup from the chicken and sweetcorn soup in my first book, *Simply Chinese*. However, I always have spinach in my fridge and freezer, which gives this soup a lovely appearance with the flecks of green. I also added some silken tofu cubes (my favourite) to give this warming soup additional protein and texture.

INGREDIENTS

chicken or vegetable stock (homemade or store-bought)	2 litres (68 fl oz/ 8½ cups)
fresh ginger root, peeled and sliced	30 g (1 oz)
spring onions (scallions), chopped into thirds	4
garlic, sliced	2 large cloves
salt	½ teaspoon
white pepper	¼ teaspoon
cornflour (cornstarch) paste (page 17)	approx. 3 tablespoons
eggs, beaten	4
shredded spinach	approx. 200 g (7 oz)
medium or firm regular tofu or silken tofu (homemade or store-bought), cubed	approx. 300 g (10½ oz)
sesame oil	2 teaspoons

METHOD

Pour your choice of stock into a large saucepan/soup pot, then add the ginger, spring onion, garlic, salt and pepper and allow to boil for 10 minutes.

Add about 3 tablespoons of cornflour paste and let the soup come to a boil again. If the soup is not thick enough for you, add more cornflour paste a tablespoon at a time and let it come to the boil each time.

Use a wooden spoon to swirl the soup, then slowly drizzle in the beaten eggs in a steady stream and keep stirring – this will add flecks of egg through the soup.

Next add the shredded spinach, tofu cubes and sesame oil and let the soup bubble for another couple of minutes to heat through. Now season to taste with more salt and pepper.

TOP TIPS

- This soup freezes well, but will become more watery when defrosted, so bring to the boil again and add a couple of tablespoons of cornflour paste to thicken.

- Add chicken, ham or prawns (shrimp) to bulk up the soup and make it a heartier dish. I love spooning it over a bowl of rice.

Hot Pot

SERVES: 8
PREP: 1 hour (if making soup base from scratch)

Hot pot was a big party sharing meal in our house. It was a simple way to cater to people's food needs because everyone chose their own raw ingredients and added them to the hot pot. I loved having this for someone's birthday or just because I love it! I enjoy eating lots of different things and having a hot pot in the comfort of your own home is even better in my opinion.

INGREDIENTS: OPTION 1

You will need the following ingredients if cooking the soup base from scratch:

SOUP BASE

Use my Drunken Chicken Soup (page 80) or make a plainer one by leaving out the Shaoxing wine.

MEAT AND FISH

Use thin slices of raw meat such as beef steak, salmon or other fish fillets, prawns (shrimp), scallops, squid, crab sticks, octopus balls and my homemade fish balls (page 26).

VEGETABLES

Use an assortment of mushrooms (fresh rehydrated shiitake, rehydrated wood ear), pak choi (bok choi), spinach, watercress, Chinese cabbage, lotus root, sweet potato, daikon (mooli) and sweetcorn.

TOFU

Use tofu puffs or sheets, or my Homemade Tofu (page 111).

CARBOHYDRATES

Try noodles (rice-based noodles are the best as they hold their shape), rehydrated rice cakes or my Traditional Dumplings (page 126).

DIPPING SAUCES

Use light soy sauce, my Spicy Chilli Oil (page 122) or homemade satay sauce (page 106), or a black vinegar-based sauce.

INGREDIENTS: OPTION 2

If you are not making the soup base from scratch, you can buy premade soup stock from Asian supermarkets specifically for hot pot. In our family we have two pots going, one for a spicy soup and one for a plainer version.

You will then need two ingredients from each of the categories for Option 1 – meat, vegetables, tofu, carbohydrates and dipping sauces. You can always add more, depending on how hungry you are.

METHOD

Heat the soup base/store-bought hot pot stock in a large soup pot placed in the middle of the table on top of a portable induction hob or gas camping stove, so everyone can choose their ingredients for cooking in the pot.

Set out all the different ingredients on plates or bowls around the hot pot ready for people to dunk in their food of choice.

Add the dipping sauces to large bowls with teaspoons, so people can spoon them into their own bowls.

Once the soup is boiling, each person can add their ingredients to the pot. Make sure the ingredients boil for at least 30–60 seconds, especially when raw meat or seafood are used.

Then use a slotted spoon, wire ladles or chopsticks to retrieve the cooked food from the pot.

TOP TIP

- Make sure all the ingredients for the hot pot are ready to go at once, as there is nothing more frustrating than when something isn't ready and you are waiting to eat! So while the soup base is heating through, prepare the other ingredients and have them ready on the table for sharing.

Drunken Chicken Soup

SERVES: 4–6
PREP: 10 minutes
COOK: 1 hour

As a family we used to go to a local Chinese restaurant in Belfast and they served drunken chicken soup on its own or as one of the soup bases for their hot pot. We ordered this often as a family and it was very warming and had a distinctive taste. I have simplified the recipe, but I show you how to maximise the flavours. There should be at least another two herbal ingredients – angelica root and ginseng – to make this into a truly authentic soup. These transform the soup into a very nourishing food for women during their confinement period post-partum. Ginger is also a key aromatic used in dishes for new mothers. Let's just say I ate a lot of ginger after my little ones were born!

INGREDIENTS

chicken legs	4
sesame oil	2 tablespoons
fresh ginger root, peeled and sliced	40 g (1½ oz)
garlic cloves, sliced	4
spring onions (scallions), chopped into quarters	4
Shaoxing wine	250 ml (8 fl oz/ 1 cup)
water	2.5 litres (84 fl oz/generous 10½ cups)
chicken stock powder (optional)	1 teaspoon
goji berries	4 tablespoons
dried red dates, cut in half (optional)	6
salt and white pepper	

METHOD

Pat the chicken legs dry with some paper towels.

Add the sesame oil to a large soup pot, then fry off the chicken legs to brown them – about 3–4 minutes on each side. You may have to fry two legs at a time if the pot is too small. Lift the legs out onto a plate.

Add the ginger, garlic and spring onions to the pot and fry for another couple of minutes until the aromas are released.

Return the chicken legs to the pot, then pour in the Shaoxing wine to deglaze. Pour in 2.5 litres (84 fl oz/generous 10½ cups) of water and add the chicken stock powder (if using).

Then add the goji berries, red dates (if using), ¼ teaspoon of white pepper and a pinch of salt. Put the lid on.

Bring the soup to the boil for 10 minutes, then simmer for a further 50 minutes. Season to taste with salt and pepper.

TOP TIPS

- If you have any leftover chicken from the hot pot, strip the meat off the bone and stir it through my Spinach Egg Drop Soup recipe (page 76) or use it for fried rice.

- This soup is also a great way to jazz up a bowl of rice if you cannot be bothered to cook dinner!

- The soup tastes even better the next day and will keep for four days in the fridge. Always bring the soup to a roaring boil before serving to kill off any bacteria.

RICE & NOODLES

05

五

飯
麵

Feasts usually end with rice or noodles to ensure everyone feels full. Rice is a staple in Chinese culture in the farming areas and especially in Southern China. Some rice superstitions include: not running out of rice, as this signifies no more luck; eating every grain of rice, so your future spouse will not have blemishes; and always having an abundance of rice at Chinese family feasts. Noodles are a must during Chinese New Year, representing longevity, with each strand consumed unbroken to avoid bad luck.

CHAPTER FIVE

五 五

THE MENU

CHILLI AND BLACK
BEAN MUSSELS
WITH NOODLES
84

SALMON
FRIED RICE
86

SHREDDED CHICKEN
AND CHOOT
CHOI NOODLES
88

QUICK CONGEE
91

CRISPY CHILLI EGG
NOODLE BOWL
92

'NO CLAYPOT' RICE
94

YUNG CHOW
FRIED RICE
96

CHOW MEIN
99

THE PERFECT
BOILED RICE
100

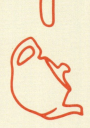

Chilli and Black Bean Mussels with Noodles

SERVES: 6
PREP: 25 minutes
COOK: 20 minutes

I first made this dish during lockdown as my children were really enjoying mussels, and I decided to bulk it up with some noodles to stretch out the dish. I hold back on the amount of chilli I use in this dish for my family, but I do love the kick it adds.

INGREDIENTS

fresh mussels	1 kg (2 lb 4 oz)
dried egg noodle nests	6, each weighing about 60–75 g (2–2½ oz)
Chinese dried fermented black beans	3 tablespoons
vegetable oil	1 tablespoon
fresh ginger root, peeled and sliced into rounds	30 g (1 oz)
large spring onions (scallions), 4 chopped into 7.5 cm (3 in) pieces and 2 finely sliced for garnishing	6
large garlic cloves, finely chopped	4
large chilli, finely sliced (optional)	1
light soy sauce	2 tablespoons
sesame oil	2 teaspoons
sugar (optional)	1 teaspoon
cornflour (cornstarch) paste (page 17)	1 tablespoon
water	approx. 200 ml (7 fl oz/scant 1 cup)
salt and white pepper	

TOP TIP

- Fermented black beans (fermented soy beans) can be bought in your local Chinese supermarket or online. They are very inexpensive and any that are left over will keep in your freezer for ages. Make sure you don't buy Mexican black beans, which are completely different!

METHOD

To prepare the mussels, clean each one on the outside with a scourer/brush. Check for 'beards' around the seams, pulling them out and discarding these 'hairy' pieces. Throw away any ones with broken shells, they are spoiled.

Put the mussels in a bowl of cold water and allow to sit for about 20 minutes, so the grit can be rinsed out. Give the mussels another rinse in the bowl under a cold running tap. Then use a colander to drain off the water. Tap any unclosed mussels on the work surface: if they close, they are still alive, but otherwise discard them.

Prepare the noodles by rehydrating in cold water for at least 30 minutes until the strands are separable, then drain, pat dry and leave on top of some paper towels to remove excess water. (You can also use fresh egg noodles.)

Fry off the ginger and the four chopped spring onions for a couple of minutes. Add the garlic and chilli (if using) to the wok/pan and fry for about a minute until everything becomes fragrant.

Next, rehydrate the black beans by soaking in just enough boiling water to cover them for 15 minutes, then pour off the excess water just before using.

Add the rehydrated black beans without the soaking water to the wok/pan followed by the soy sauce, sesame oil and sugar (if using), and allow to simmer for a couple of minutes. Then stir in the cornflour paste.

Toss the mussels into the wok/pan and add approximately 200 ml (7 fl oz/scant 1 cup) of water. Cover with a lid or some tin foil and cook for at least 5 minutes, shaking the wok/pan occasionally. Keep checking to see if all the mussel shells have opened.

Finally, add the rehydrated noodles to the wok/pan and mix everything together. Allow to come up to the boil for a couple of minutes until the sauce is absorbed by the noodles.

Season to taste with salt and pepper. You may wish to add more soy sauce or sesame oil as well or even more chilli.

Before serving, garnish with the sliced spring onions.

Salmon Fried Rice

SERVES: 4
PREP: 10 minutes
COOK: 20 minutes

This is a midweek classic in my household. It uses up leftover veg for my fried rice and the addition of the salmon gives a super nutrient-dense protein to my children's diet. It is easy to make, and my two little ones love it as it is so tasty.

INGREDIENTS

vegetable oil, for frying	
eggs, beaten	4
salmon fillets, skin on (my preference)	400 g (14 oz)
small onion, finely sliced	1
garlic cloves, finely chopped	2
fresh ginger root, peeled and finely chopped	30 g (1 oz)
sesame oil	1 teaspoon
frozen peas	1 handful
medium carrot, peeled and grated	1
courgette (zucchini), grated	1
cold cooked basmati rice (or the microwavable packets of rice)	500 g (1 lb 2 oz)
light soy sauce	2 tablespoons
oyster sauce	2 tablespoons
sea salt and white pepper	

TO GARNISH

spring onions (scallions), finely sliced	2
red chilli, finely sliced	1

METHOD

Heat 1 tablespoon of vegetable oil in a wok or large frying pan, then fry off the beaten egg like an omelette. Remove the egg from the heat and transfer to a plate just before it is fully cooked and set (it will continue cooking when removed from the heat).

Add another tablespoon of oil to the wok/pan, then fry off the salmon, skin side down, over a high heat. Fry for 4 minutes, then flip and cook for another couple of minutes on the other side. Remove the salmon from the heat, peel off the skin and sprinkle the flesh with a little sea salt. Transfer to the plate with the egg. Do not wash the wok/pan as there will be residual oil and the salmon will also have released some oil.

Fry off the onion in the wok/pan until slightly soft, then add the garlic, ginger and sesame oil, and let the aromas be released.

Add the carrot and courgette to the wok/pan and toss for a couple of minutes. Then add the cooked rice, breaking it down with a wooden spoon, followed by the soy sauce.

Return the egg, salmon and peas to the wok/pan, and break the egg into smaller pieces with the wooden spoon.

To finish, add the oyster sauce and season with salt and pepper to taste. You may also want to add more soy sauce and sesame oil, as required.

Garnish with the spring onion and chilli before serving.

TOP TIP

- I love frying off the salmon skin until it is super crisp (no need for extra oil) and then crunching it over the rice! I hate waste, so this is one of my favourite things to do when I have fish skin – it also adds great texture to any dish.

Shredded Chicken and Choot Choi Noodles

SERVES: 2
PREP: 15 minutes
COOK: 25 minutes

I remember eating this a lot as a snack after swimming (yes, it was a snack, as I would have eaten dinner at about 4:30pm after school before going to swimming training at 6:30pm for 2 hours). I guess this was an easy dish for Mum to make for us but also filling. I have such lovely memories of eating this bowl of noodles. Choot choi is pickled snow cabbage in Cantonese but you can use any Chinese pickled vegetables.

INGREDIENTS

chicken thighs or breast, cut into thin strips	300 g (10½ oz)
dried rice vermicelli	100 g (3½ oz) (2 nests)
vegetable oil, for frying	
choot choi (or other Chinese pickled vegetable), drained	150 g (5½ oz)
sugar	½ teaspoon
cornflour (cornstarch) paste (page 17)	1 teaspoon

MARINADE

cornflour (cornstarch)	2 teaspoons
light soy sauce	2 teaspoons
sesame oil	1 teaspoon
Shaoxing wine	1 teaspoon

BROTH

water	400 ml (14 fl oz/ generous 1½ cups)
chicken stock powder	2 teaspoons
light soy sauce	1 teaspoon
sesame oil	1 teaspoon
white pepper	½ teaspoon

METHOD

Mix all the ingredients for the marinade in a bowl, then marinate the chicken strips for 15 minutes.

Soak the vermicelli in a bowl of cold water (enough to cover the noodles) for 15 minutes, then strain with a colander and set aside.

To make the broth, bring the water to a boil with all the other ingredients in a cooking pot or saucepan, boil for 5 minutes and then simmer for a further 10 minutes.

Heat 1 tablespoon of vegetable oil in a wok or large frying pan over a high heat, then fry off the chicken strips for about 5 minutes until cooked through and browned.

Add the pickled vegetables and sugar to the wok/pan and fry for a further 5 minutes. Pour in approximately 125 ml (4 fl oz/½ cup) of water, add the cornflour paste and bring to the boil to thicken the sauce. Taste and adjust the seasoning – if you think the sauce is too sharp, add another pinch of sugar.

To serve, divide the vermicelli between two bowls, then pour the boiling broth over the noodles (you may want less, so hold back). Spoon the chicken and pickled vegetables over the noodles and drizzle with more sesame oil if you wish.

Enjoy this comforting bowl of hot noodle soup right away!

TOP TIPS

- You can also use beef steak or pork loin/fillet/shoulder instead of the chicken – just use whatever you have to hand.

- I also like to marinate more meat than I need and keep portions of it in the freezer ready to be reheated and used later.

- This is the same pickled cabbage I used in the Beef Mince and Choot Choi recipe (page 67).

Quick Congee

SERVES: 2
PREP: 5 minutes
COOK: 30 minutes

This is a great recipe that uses leftover rice and gives you a very warming bowl of savoury rice pudding/congee, which is served in Hong Kong street markets and dim sum. From scratch it takes about an hour, but this version is super quick and takes under 30 minutes. Mum used to make a big pot of congee when we were sick as it was very easy to eat.

INGREDIENTS

leftover cooked rice	500 g (1 lb 2 oz)
water	1.25 litres (40 fl oz/ 5¼ cups)
chicken stock powder	2 tablespoons
white pepper	¼ teaspoon
pinch of salt	

ACCOMPANIMENT IDEAS

Salted Chicken Eggs (page 46)
Spicy Chilli Oil (page 122)
red fermented bean curd/tofu
soy sauce
sliced spring onions (scallions)

METHOD

Add the cooked rice, water, chicken stock powder, pepper and salt to a large saucepan and mix well. Bring to the boil for 5 minutes, then lower the temperature to a medium heat and simmer for approximately 25 minutes.

The congee should have a thick, porridge-like consistency – if you would prefer it more fluid, add more water. Season to taste with more salt and pepper.

Serve the congee with whatever accompaniment takes your fancy. I like to steam a homemade salted duck/chicken egg and scoop the contents into the congee, mix it all together and enjoy each mouthful with bursts of salty egg flavour through the soft creamy congee.

TOP TIPS

- Add any leftover meat you have from other dishes to bulk out this dish and give it extra flavour.
- You can use frozen leftover cooked rice.

Crispy Chilli Egg Noodle Bowl

SERVES: 1
PREP: 5 minutes
COOK: 10 minutes

This is an easy recipe to make whenever you are rushing. It uses a packet of instant noodles but still packs in lots of flavour with a few ingredients. I add frankfurter octopuses to garnish the bowl for a bit of fun.

INGREDIENTS

1 packet of instant ramen noodles with the dried soup sachet packet (or use any noodles and make half the broth from my Shredded Chicken and Choot Choi Noodles recipe on page 88)

frankfurters	1 or 2

CHILLI EGGS

eggs	2
Spicy Chilli Oil (page 122)	2 tablespoons

ACCOMPANIMENT IDEAS

Spicy Chilli Oil (page 122)
blanched vegetables, such as pak choi (bok choi), broccoli, spinach and Chinese cabbage
red fermented bean curd/tofu
soy sauce
sliced spring onions (scallions)
sesame oil
sesame seeds

METHOD

To prepare the frankfurter octopuses, cut the frankfurters into halves or thirds, then use a sharp knife to cut through each piece two-thirds of the way lengthways (leaving one-third for the head). Rotate the piece of frankfurter by 90 degrees and cut again so each piece has four 'legs'. Then cut each of the four legs to make eight legs. Just be careful when cutting, as the frankfurters can break easily.

Boil some water in a cooking pot or saucepan and add the frankfurters. The legs will curl up within 2 minutes and start to look like an octopus. Remove the frankfurter octopuses carefully with a slotted spoon and set aside.

Put the noodles in the same pot/pan, boil for 5 minutes and then strain with a colander. If you are using vegetables as an accompaniment, you can lift the noodles out with a slotted spoon and blanch the vegetables in the hot water.

While the noodles are cooking, prepare the chilli eggs. Heat 2 tablespoons of chilli oil (without the sediment) in a wok or large frying pan over a high heat and wait until the oil is sizzling. Then crack in the eggs – you should immediately see the edges bubbling up and becoming crispy. Spoon the oil over the egg until the whites are set (about 2–3 minutes).

To serve, pour 200 ml (7 fl oz/scant 1 cup) of boiling water into a large bowl, then mix in the sachet of soup powder that came with the noodles. Then add the noodles and top with the frankfurter octopuses and vegetables (if using). Slide the crispy eggs into the bowl and spoon over some of the chilli oil sediment.

Top with sesame seeds, spring onions or anything that takes your fancy.

TOP TIP

• Top the noodle bowl with anything you have in the freezer, fridge or cupboard, such as ham, chicken, prawns (shrimp) and tofu.

'No Claypot' Rice

SERVES: 4
PREP: 15 minutes
COOK: 45 minutes

I love clay pot rice, or *bo zai fan*, and it is very popular at dim sum, as the clay pot gives the rice a crispy bottom, which is characteristic of the dish and absolutely delicious. However, I do not own a clay pot, so I have found a different way to achieve the crispy rice bottom.

INGREDIENTS

basmati rice	300 g (10½ oz)
vegetable oil, for frying	
salt and white pepper	

CHICKEN AND SHIITAKE MUSHROOMS TOPPING

chicken thighs, finely sliced	400 g (14 oz)
fresh shiitake mushrooms, finely sliced	100 g (3½ oz) or 20 g (¾ oz) dried shiitake mushrooms (rehydrated to give approx. 100 g/3½ oz)
cornflour (cornstarch)	1 teaspoon
light soy sauce	1 tablespoon
Shaoxing wine	1 teaspoon
oyster sauce	2 tablespoons
white pepper	¼ teaspoon

CHINESE SAUSAGE TOPPING

Chinese sausage, blanched quickly in hot water (for about 30 seconds) and the skin peeled off and thinly sliced	2 links (approx. 100 g (3½ oz)/ 50 g (1¾ oz) each)

SAUCE

water	approx. 250 ml (8 fl oz/1 cup)
finely chopped garlic	1 teaspoon
oyster sauce	3 tablespoons
chicken stock powder	1 teaspoon
cornflour (cornstarch) paste (page 17)	1 tablespoon
sesame oil	1 teaspoon

METHOD

Rinse the rice in a bowl with cold water three times to remove some of the starch, then strain and set aside.

For the chicken and mushroom topping, add all the cornflour, soy sauce, Shaoxing wine, oyster sauce and white pepper to a bowl, then marinate the chicken and shiitake mushrooms for at least 15 minutes.

To make the Chinese sausage topping, heat 1 tablespoon of vegetable oil in a large saucepan or cast-iron casserole dish (Dutch oven) over a high heat, then fry off the sausage for about 2 minutes to brown. Remove the sausage and set aside.

Add another tablespoon of oil to the same pan/dish, then fry off the rinsed rice for a couple of minutes. Pour in approximately 500 ml (17 fl oz/generous 2 cups) of water, then cook over a low to medium heat with no lid until the water has evaporated to the level of the rice (about 10–15 minutes).

Place the Chinese sausage and marinaded chicken and mushroom on top of the rice in a single layer – try not to overlap the meat as you want it to cook evenly – then put the lid on the pan/dish. The larger the surface area of your pan/dish, the easier it will be for you to spread the meat evenly in one layer to cook and the quicker the food will cook.

Ensure the stovetop is at the lowest heat setting and steam for 10 minutes (without lifting the lid). Then check, as the rice and chicken may need another 5 minutes to cook.

Now it's time to crisp up the bottom of the rice. Increase the heat under the pan/dish and remove the lid. You should be able to smell the rice burning and crackling a little. It will take about 5–10 minutes to brown the rice – to check, scrape up some of the rice from the bottom of the pot. Heat for longer until you have the desired crispy bottomed rice.

Finally, add all the ingredients for the sauce to a small saucepan and mix well. Bring to the boil and keep stirring for about 4–5 minutes.

Pour the sauce over the dish and serve with steamed vegetables of your choice. Taste and season accordingly.

TOP TIP

- You can make the whole dish in a rice cooker, by adding in the toppings at the half-cooked rice stage (you should know the timings on your rice cooker – each one is different). My rice cooker takes 25 minutes to fully cook rice, so at approx. 12 minutes I add in the toppings. Then scoop out a portion of the rice (try to get a good portion of the rice out with some topping on top). Heat up a pan with some oil to a high heat and place the scoop of rice in and allow it to sizzle and become crispy on the bottom.

Yung Chow Fried Rice

SERVES: 2
PREP: 10 minutes
COOK: 15 minutes

The title for this dish comes from the name of the region from which it originates (Yangzhou) and it is a popular rice dish for special occasions. It usually includes a combination of meats, which would have reflected wealth, but this 'special' fried rice has morphed in our modern society into a dish ordered in takeaways. I frequently make variations of this as it lends itself to using up leftovers.

INGREDIENTS

vegetable oil, for frying	
beaten eggs	2
small onion, finely diced	1
small carrot, peeled and finely diced	1
grated fresh ginger root	2 teaspoons
grated garlic	1 teaspoon
white pepper	¼ teaspoon
salt	¼ teaspoon
sugar	⅛ teaspoon
leftover cooked chicken (White Cut Chicken (page 52) Drunken Chicken Soup (page 80)), diced	50 g (1¾ oz)
Traditional Char Siu Pork (page 59), diced	50 g (1¾ oz)
raw king prawns (shrimp), shelled, deveined and chopped into 4 pieces each	50 g (1¾ oz)
leftover cooked basmati rice (see The Perfect Boiled Rice, page 100)	250 g (9 oz)
spring onions (scallions), plus extra to garnish, finely sliced	25 g (1 oz)
light soy sauce	1½ tablespoons
frozen peas	1 small handful
sesame oil	1 teaspoon

METHOD

Heat 1 tablespoon of vegetable oil in a wok or large frying pan, then fry off the beaten egg like an omelette. Remove the egg from the heat and transfer to a plate just before it is fully cooked and set (it will keep cooking after it is removed from the heat).

Heat another tablespoon of oil in the same wok/pan over a high heat and fry off the onion and carrot with a splash of water for 2–3 minutes. Then add the ginger and garlic, white pepper, salt and sugar and fry for a further minute until aromatic.

Next add the chicken and char siu to the wok/pan and fry to heat through for about 1 minute. Add the prawns and toss, then put on the lid for 1 minute to cook the prawns through.

Add the rice, spring onion and the cooked eggs, breaking these down with a wooden spoon, then add the soy sauce and cook for 2–3 minutes – you will hear it sizzle.

Toss in the frozen peas and stir through – they will defrost in about a minute in the heat of the rice.

Finish off with a drizzle of sesame oil around the edges of the wok to activate the aromas.

Season to taste with salt and pepper and garnish with the remaining spring onions.

TOP TIP

- Using up leftover meats makes a very delicious yung chow (special) fried rice. You also don't need exact measures of each meat, so just use whatever you have.

- If you do not have leftover cooked basmati rice you can use a packet of microwavable rice.

Chow Mein

SERVES: 4
PREP: 30 minutes
COOK: 10 minutes

I am often asked for a noodle/chow mein dish, and this is my foolproof recipe for a very tasty chow mein to accompany other dishes or just on its own. It can be jazzed up with different meats and vegetables.

INGREDIENTS

dried egg noodles	350 g (12 oz)
vegetable oil, for frying	
small onion, finely sliced	1
bean sprouts	150 g (5½ oz)
chicken or vegetable stock	1 teaspoon
salt	½ teaspoon
sugar	½ teaspoon
white pepper	¼ teaspoon
dark soy sauce	2 tablespoons
sesame oil	1 teaspoon

METHOD

Prepare the noodles by rehydrating in cold water for at least 30 minutes until the strands are separable, then drain, pat dry and leave on top of some paper towels to remove excess water. (You can use fresh egg noodles too, if you wish.)

Heat 2 tablespoons of vegetable oil in a wok or large frying pan over a high heat, then fry off the onion and bean sprouts for 2–3 minutes. There will be a little bit of charring.

Then add the rehydrated noodles to the wok/frying pan and fry for a couple of minutes. Sprinkle the chicken or vegetable stock powder, salt, sugar and white pepper over the noodles, onions and bean sprouts, and toss together.

Add 2 tablespoons of dark soy sauce to the wok/pan, then fry for a further 5 minutes to give the noodles lots of flavour. Then drizzle the sesame oil around the edges of the wok to extract as much of its flavour as possible.

TOP TIP

- Add leftover meats and vegetables to this dish to make it a full meal instead of just a side – it is so versatile!

The Perfect Boiled Rice

SERVES: 4
COOK: 20–25 minutes

I am always being asked for a boiled rice recipe, so here it is. The evaporation method I show you here will give you perfect rice every time and it also does not stick to the bottom of the pot! Only use basmati, Thai or jasmine rice, and not American long grain rice or short grain rice because it is a completely different grain and not used in Chinese cooking.

INGREDIENTS

raw basmati, Thai or jasmine rice	200 g (7 oz/1 cup)
cold tap water	

METHOD

Add the rice to a saucepan, rinse in cold water and pour off the cloudy, starchy water. Repeat this three times. Shake the pot from side to side on a flat surface, so the rice levels out.

Then add enough cold water to the pan, so that when the top of your index finger touches the top of the rice the water reaches your first knuckle.

Bring the water to a boil, then reduce to a simmer and put the lid on. Check on the rice and once the water has nearly evaporated, turn off the heat. You are looking for holes in the rice due to the bubbling of the liquid – that shows it's time to turn off the heat and put the lid back on. This steams the rice.

You now have perfect fluffy rice.

TOP TIPS

- Cool the rice quickly and store in the fridge for up to four days or in the freezer for up to a month.

- You can use any leftover rice for fried rice dishes, such as Salmon Fried Rice (page 86) and Yung Chow Fried Rice (page 96), as well as my Quick Congee (page 91).

VEGETABLES

06

六

蔬菜

When I was growing up, Mum made sure there was at least one vegetable dish served with our meals for the vitamins and minerals and just because they are 'healthy' and 'nutritious'. The word for vegetable in Cantonese is *choi* which has an auspicious ring because it sounds like wealth and fortune. Therefore, vegetables are considered a must for special occasions because all their names have 'choi' at the end.

CHAPTER SIX

THE MENU

THE MENU

SPICY CUCUMBER SALAD
105

MIXED VEGETABLE SATAY
106

FERMENTED BEAN CURD GREEN BEANS
108

HOMEMADE TOFU
111

GARLICKY TENDERSTEM BROCCOLI
113

MIXED VEGETABLE AND CRISPY TOFU STIR-FRY
114

SPICY LOTUS ROOT STIR-FRY
116

LOTUS ROOT CRISPS
119

STEAMED SILKEN TOFU
120

SPICY CHILLI OIL
122

Spicy Cucumber Salad

SERVES: 4
PREP: 20 minutes

There are many variations of a cucumber salad, here I have created a very simple no fuss recipe. You can omit the chilli oil from this cucumber salad, but I love the kick it gives it! I love adding it to rice and noodle bowls and even snacking on the pieces of cucumber straight out of the jar.

INGREDIENTS

large cucumber, topped, tailed and finely sliced into circles	1
salt	1 teaspoon
sugar	1 teaspoon
rice wine vinegar	4 teaspoons
light soy sauce	1 teaspoon
sesame oil	2 teaspoons
Spicy Chilli Oil (page 122)	2 tablespoons

METHOD

Layer the cucumber slices on a plate and sprinkle over ½ teaspoon of salt, then add another layer of cucumber and sprinkle with another ½ teaspoon of salt. Mix with your hand and leave for 15 minutes.

Strain off the liquid from the cucumber, then pat dry with a couple of pieces of paper towel to remove excess salt.

Mix the sugar, rice wine vinegar, soy sauce and sesame oil in a bowl to make a dressing for the salad. Toss the cucumber in the dressing, then taste and adjust the seasoning – you may want it sharper, so add more rice wine vinegar.

Finally, add a couple of tablespoons of homemade spicy chilli oil for extra flavour.

TOP TIP

- You can keep this salad in a jar in the fridge for a couple of days.

Mixed Vegetable Satay

SERVES: 4
PREP: 10 minutes
COOK: 30 minutes

Satay sauce is so addictive with the peanut butter being the really moreish element. I have developed this recipe using normal household ingredients instead of a ready-made paste, and it is super easy to make.

INGREDIENTS

vegetable oil, for frying	

SATAY SAUCE

large onion, finely diced	1
spring onions (scallions), finely sliced	4
curry powder (mild/medium/hot)	3 tablespoons
large chilli, deseeded and finely chopped	1 (more if you want the satay spicier)
smooth peanut butter	4 heaped tablespoons
dark brown sugar	4 tablespoons
coconut milk	400 g (14 oz)
sesame oil	1 teaspoon
cornflour (cornstarch) paste (page 17) (optional)	1–2 tablespoons
salt and white pepper	

VEGETABLES

large (bell) pepper, deseeded and sliced	1
mangetout (snow peas) or sugar snap peas, sliced on the diagonal	1 packet (approx. 300 g/10½ oz)
mushrooms, sliced	handful
baby corn, sliced on the diagonal	1 packet (approx. 300 g/10½ oz)
chicken or vegetable stock cube	1
boiling water	approx. 500 ml (17 fl oz/generous 2 cups)
spring onions (scallions), sliced on the diagonal, for garnishing	2

METHOD

To make the satay sauce, fry off the onion and spring onion in a saucepan in a little vegetable oil until softened. Add the curry powder and fry for about a minute until it becomes fragrant (make sure it doesn't burn).

Add the chilli, peanut butter and sugar to the pan and cook for a couple of minutes (it will be very thick), then add the coconut milk. Season to taste with salt and pepper, as required, then add the sesame oil.

To cook the vegetables, heat approximately 2 tablespoons of vegetable oil in another wok or large frying pan, then fry off the pepper, mangetout or sugar snap peas, mushrooms and baby corn. Add a large splash of water into the pan and crumble in the stock cube (it adds extra flavour), and then allow the vegetables to cook for about 2–3 minutes.

Mix the satay sauce into the vegetables in the wok/pan. If the sauce is too thick, add some of the boiling water to thin it out. You may not need all of the water; but I know some like 'a lot' of sauce to go over their rice/noodles.

Taste again and season with salt and pepper, as required. Toss in the spring onions and serve with some basmati rice.

TOP TIPS

- Freeze the sauce, if you wish – it will keep for a month in the freezer.

- You can add prawns (shrimp) or a meat alternative to increase the protein of this recipe. You can also use any vegetables in your larder.

Fermented Bean Curd Green Beans

SERVES: 2
PREP: 10 minutes
COOK: 20 minutes

Fermented bean curd is a really popular Chinese cooking ingredient and is used in a number of the recipes in the book. It is the closest thing the Chinese have to cheese. It comes in two forms – white fermented or red fermented (the red version uses red rice yeast, which gives a more intense flavour and colouring). I have focused on red fermented bean curd, which is used in a lot of meat dishes, for this book. This recipe is usually made with an Asian vegetable called 'morning glory', but this isn't always easy to get hold of if you don't have access to an Asian supermarket. However, if you have bought a jar of fermented bean curd, then make this dish with vegetables you can buy locally.

METHOD

Add the green beans with 4 tablespoons of water to a wok or large frying pan, put on the lid and bring to a boil for 2–3 minutes (the beans will steam). Remove the beans and set aside.

Dry the wok/pan and add 1 teaspoon of vegetable oil, then fry off the mashed bean curd with the garlic and chilli (if using) and a pinch each of sugar and pepper for a couple of minutes until you can smell the aromas being released.

Return the green beans to the wok/pan, then toss to coat in the sauce. Season with salt and pepper to taste, then drizzle over the sesame oil to serve.

INGREDIENTS

green beans, topped and tailed	250 g (9 oz)
vegetable oil, for frying	
fermented red bean curd, mashed with 2 teaspoons of liquid from the jar	3 cubes
finely chopped garlic	1 heaped teaspoon (about 1 large clove)
red chilli, sliced (optional)	1
sugar	pinch
sesame oil	1 teaspoon
salt and white pepper	

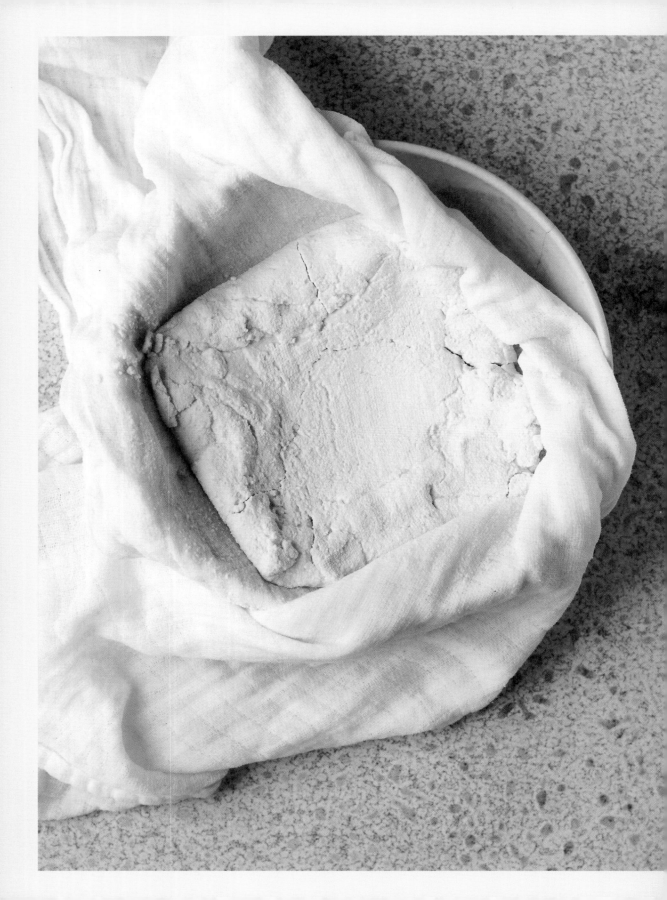

Homemade Tofu

MAKES: 1 small block (approx. 200–250 g/7–9 oz)
COOK: 15 minutes
SETTING TIME: 2–4 hours

Having made soy milk, I stumbled across a number of recipes that said it was really easy to make tofu from soy milk. Therefore, I thought I would investigate ... and it is! Hot soy milk plus an acid (lemon juice or a vinegar) can produce a wonderful block of tofu. You need a good-quality soy milk, so homemade soy milk is the best – if it is very weak-tasting soy milk, then it will not coagulate to form the tofu. The process is just like cheese making. My preferred choice of acid is rice wine vinegar because I always have a bottle in my cupboard.

INGREDIENTS

unsweetened soy milk (page 160)	1 litre (34 fl oz/ 4¼ cups)
rice wine vinegar or lemon juice	approx. 1½ tablespoons

METHOD

Heat the soy milk to a gentle simmer in a large cooking pot. Add the rice wine vinegar or lemon juice and stir until the mixture starts to curdle. Turn off the heat once the whey is transparent – it is the curds you want for the tofu.

Place a large sieve in a bowl lined with a piece of muslin (cheesecloth) and drain the soy mixture to collect the pieces of tofu. Do this when the mixture is still hot. Discard the liquid whey and squeeze the excess liquid out of the curds.

Now wrap the tofu in the piece of muslin and place in a container with a weight on top. If you do not work with the curds when hot, they will not hold in a block form as well and will crumble.

After a couple of hours, you will have soft-set tofu. For firmer tofu, place in the fridge for 4 hours.

Steam the tofu as a block or cut it up and add to stir-fries and soups. You can also deep-fry the tofu.

TOP TIP

- You can also freeze the tofu for up to a month or keep it in the fridge for a week in an airtight container.

Garlicky Tenderstem Broccoli

SERVES: 2–4
PREP: 5 minutes
COOK: 10 minutes

This is a super-simple vegetable dish with lots of flavour, and you can switch up the vegetable if you have something different in your larder or fridge. It is a very versatile sauce.

INGREDIENTS

vegetable oil	1 tablespoon
garlic, finely chopped	2 large garlic cloves
chicken or vegetable stock powder	½ teaspoon
light soy sauce	1 teaspoon
oyster sauce (or vegetarian version)	1 tablespoon
water	200 ml (7 fl oz/ scant 1 cup)
tenderstem broccoli or green beans, trimmed	250 g (9 oz)
cornflour (cornstarch) paste (page 17) (optional)	2 teaspoons
salt and white pepper	

METHOD

Heat the vegetable oil in a wok or large frying pan, then fry the garlic until fragrant over a high heat, but be careful not to let it burn.

Add the stock powder, light soy sauce, oyster sauce, ¼ teaspoon of white pepper and the water to the wok/pan, then allow to simmer for a couple of minutes.

Next add the broccoli or green beans to the wok/pan and toss through the sauce. Put the lid on and steam for 5 minutes until the vegetables are tender. Season to taste with salt and pepper.

If you would like a thicker sauce, add a couple of teaspoons of cornflour paste, bring the dish up to the boil and the sauce will thicken.

Mixed Vegetable and Crispy Tofu Stir-Fry

SERVES: 2–4
PREP: 10 minutes
COOK: 10 minutes

This recipe uses leftover vegetables and other ingredients to make a tasty stir-fry. You could use leftover tofu, green vegetables such as pak choi (bok choi) or the beansprouts from my Traditional Spring Roll recipe (page 128).

INGREDIENTS

tofu (shop-bought or homemade, page 111)	approx. 250 g (9 oz)
cornflour (cornstarch)	2 tablespoons
vegetable oil, for frying	
fresh ginger root, peeled and grated	20 g (¾ oz)
mushrooms, sliced	300 g (10½ oz)
vegetable or chicken stock powder	1 teaspoon
light soy sauce	3 teaspoons
oyster sauce (or vegetarian version)	3 tablespoons
bean sprouts	300 g (10½ oz)
pak choi (bok choi), trimmed, stalk ends sliced across into chunks, leafy top left intact	1
cornflour (cornstarch) paste (page 17) (optional)	approx. 1 teaspoon
salt and white pepper	

METHOD

Chop the tofu into bite-size pieces and pat dry with some paper towels to absorb the excess moisture. Then toss the tofu in the cornflour.

Heat 3 tablespoons of vegetable oil in a wok or large frying pan, then fry off the tofu until crispy and golden on all sides. Set aside in a dish.

Fry off the ginger in the same wok/pan in 1 tablespoon of vegetable oil over a high heat for 1 minute until fragrant. Make sure the ginger doesn't burn and add a splash of water if it starts to catch.

Add the mushrooms to the wok/pan and fry for another couple of minutes. Then add the remainder of the seasoning ingredients: the stock powder, ¼ teaspoon of white pepper, the soy sauce, and oyster sauce.

Finally, add the bean sprouts and pak choi as well as the crispy tofu. Stir-fry for another couple of minutes – if you like softer vegetables, then cook for longer. Season to taste with salt and pepper.

If you would like a sauce, then add a little water to the wok/pan (liquid will also have been released from the vegetables), bringing up to the boil and thickening the sauce with a teaspoon of cornflour paste at a time.

Serve the vegetables with some rice or noodles or on their own.

TOP TIP

- Use whatever vegetables you have to hand for this recipe or add some meat of your choice – the flavours and seasoning are a good base for any dish.

Spicy Lotus Root Stir-Fry

SERVES: 2–4
PREP: 15 minutes
COOK: 10 minutes

Lotus root and wood ear mushroom add a lovely layer of texture to any meal. I will happily eat this dish on its own without any accompaniments, as I find each mouthful of sweet carrot with the crunchy, starchy lotus root, the bite of the wood ear mushroom and the lightness of the mangetout or sugar snap peas fills me up before I know it.

INGREDIENTS

VEGETABLES

dried wood ear mushroom	15 g (½ oz)
small lotus root	1 (approx. 125 g/ 4 oz)
carrot, peeled and sliced on the diagonal	100 g (3½ oz) (about 1 carrot)
mangetout (snow peas) or sugar snap peas	50 g (1¾ oz)
salt and white pepper	

SAUCE

vegetable oil	2 tablespoons
fresh ginger root, grated	15 g (½ oz)
garlic, grated	1 large garlic clove
chilli, finely sliced	1
dark soy sauce	2 tablespoons
sesame oil	1 teaspoon
vegetable or chicken stock powder	1 teaspoon
cornflour (cornstarch) paste (page 17)	1–2 tablespoons

METHOD

Soak the dried wood ear mushroom in a bowl with 250 ml (8 fl oz/1 cup) of boiling water to rehydrate for at least 15 minutes (you may need to weight it down with another bowl as it should be fully submerged). Keep the liquid to make the sauce.

Peel and top and tail the lotus root, slice into thin circles and rinse under cold water. Place the slices of lotus root in a cooking pot with approximately 150 ml (5 fl oz/scant ⅔ cup) of water, bring to the boil and steam with the lid on for 1 minute. Set aside when ready.

To make the sauce, heat 2 tablespoons of vegetable oil in a wok or large frying pan and fry off the ginger, garlic and chilli over a high heat for 1 minute until fragrant – be careful not to burn the spices and add a splash of water if they start to catch.

Add all the vegetables – the rehydrated wood ear mushroom, lotus root, carrot and mangetout or sugar snap peas – to the wok/pan, then some of the sauce ingredients: the soy sauce, sesame oil and stock powder.

Pour in approximately 125 ml (4 fl oz/½ cup) of the water used to soak the wood ear fugus and cook for a couple of minutes until the carrot and mangetout or sugar snap peas are to your liking. Season to taste with salt and pepper.

To thicken the sauce, add a tablespoon of cornflour paste at a time and bring the dish up to the boil before serving.

TOP TIP

- You can use leftover wood ear mushroom from the Chicken and Chestnuts recipe (page 49) and lotus root from the Pork and Lotus Root Soup (page 72) and Lotus Root Crisps (page 119).

Lotus Root Crisps

SERVES: 2–4
PREP: 15 minutes
COOK: 20 minutes

These are a cheap and cheerful potato crisp alternative made using leftover ingredients such as lotus root.

INGREDIENTS

small lotus root	1 (approx. 125 g/ 4 oz)
vegetable oil	1 tablespoon
salt and white pepper	

METHOD

Preheat the oven to 180°C fan (400°F).

Peel and top and tail the lotus root and rinse under cold water, then dry with some paper towel.

If you have a mandolin, finely slice the lotus root into circles 3 mm (⅛ in) thick; otherwise, use a sharp knife. The circles don't have to be exact.

Put the lotus root slices in a bowl, lightly drizzle with the vegetable oil and mix in a pinch of salt.

Now line a baking tin with some baking parchment and bake the lotus root in the oven for 15–20 minutes until golden in colour. Leave to cool for a couple of minutes, then season to taste with salt and pepper.

TOP TIP

- Try different seasonings, such as garlic powder, five-spice powder or whatever takes your fancy.

Steamed Silken Tofu

SERVES: 2–4
PREP: 20 minutes
COOK: 20 minutes

I always have a block of silken tofu in my cupboard, as it is great for when I do not have a vegetarian option for guests! It is a quick, easy and low-fuss recipe. Make sure the black beans are the Chinese fermented variety and not the Mexican ones.

INGREDIENTS

dried Chinese fermented black beans	2 tablespoons
silken tofu block	approx. 300 g (10½ oz)
large garlic cloves, finely chopped	2
ginger root, peed and finely julienned	2 tablespoons
light soy sauce	1 tablespoon
sesame oil	1 teaspoon
pinch of white pepper	

TO GARNISH

spring onions (scallions), finely sliced	2
vegetable oil	1 large tablespoon

METHOD

To prepare the fermented black beans, soak in boiling water (just enough to cover them) in a bowl for 15 minutes and then strain off the excess water just before using.

Fill the bottom section of a steamer with some cold water, insert the steaming section with the holes, put on the lid and bring the water to the boil.

Put the tofu in a heatproof dish (which will fit into the steamer). Then mix strained black beans, garlic, ginger, soy sauce, sesame oil and pepper in a bowl and pour over the tofu.

Once the water in the steamer is boiling, steam the tofu on the dish with the lid on for about 15 minutes.

Garnish the tofu with the spring onions (and even more ginger if you like). Bring the vegetable oil to the smoking point in a small saucepan, then pour over the spring onions to enhance their flavour (it will lightly fry the spring onions). The smell will be amazing! You are now ready to serve.

Spicy Chilli Oil

SERVES: 1 jar
PREP: 10 minutes
COOK: 50 minutes

This is a yummy condiment that I love adding as a side with a rice or noodle bowl. It is crunchy, sharp, sweet and very moreish – a newly updated version of my chilli oil (original version found in my *Simply Chinese* cookbook).

INGREDIENTS

sesame seeds	50 g (1¾ oz/ ⅓ cup)
peanuts	50 g (1¾ oz/ ⅓ cup)
groundnut (peanut) or vegetable oil	250 ml (8 fl oz/ 1 cup)
garlic, smashed	4 large cloves
fresh ginger root, peeled and sliced	20 g (¾ oz)
spring onions (scallions), cut into 5 cm (2 in) pieces	30 g (1 oz)
star anise	2
cinnamon stick	1
Chinese fermented black beans, rinsed and dried	75 g (2½ oz)
crushed dried hot chilli (hot pepper) flakes	2 teaspoons
chilli powder	1 teaspoon
five-spice powder	1 teaspoon
sesame oil	1 teaspoon
white pepper	1 teaspoon
salt	½ teaspoon
dark soy sauce	6 tablespoons
chicken stock powder	2 tablespoons

METHOD

Toast the sesame seeds in a dry saucepan over a low heat until they are golden and repeat for the peanuts. Set aside.

In a wok or large frying pan put in the groundnut oil or vegetable oil, garlic, ginger, spring onion, star anise and cinnamon stick, let it come up to a roaring boil. Boil for 1 minute over a high heat (make sure it is not burning, take it off the heat immediately if it is) and then simmer on low for 15 minutes until the garlic is golden in colour. Leave to cool for 10 minutes, then strain through a metal sieve to catch all the aromatics. Set the oil aside.

Add the black beans to the wok/pan along with the recently strained oil. Bring to a simmer and cook for 15–20 minutes until the popping sounds stop, which means all the moisture has evaporated from the beans.

Add the roasted peanuts and sesame seeds, chilli flakes, chilli powder, five-spice powder, sesame oil, pepper and salt to 1 large, clean jar. Then carefully pour the hot oil with the black beans into a large heatproof bowl/jar/container. Once cool, then pour the oil into the jar with the aromatics and mix.

Once the chilli oil mixture is fully cooled, add the soy sauce and chicken stock powder to the jar and mix. The oil is now ready to use. Keep in the fridge and use within a month.

TOP TIPS

- The oil can be used to enhance so many dishes or as a condiment.

DIM SUM & DUMPLINGS

07 七

點心 水餃

Dim sum translates as 'touch the heart', but the meaning of the words is derived from the word for 'appetiser'. Dim sum originated in teahouses thousands of years ago where you could enjoy bite-size dishes with an assortment of teas. Dim sum brings back so many memories: I loved seeing the trollies loaded with goodies being wheeled past and our parents allowing us to order whatever we wanted. Spring rolls, Chinese daikon cake, Malay cake, char siu puffs, dumplings, lava custard buns, frankfurter buns and mantou were all regular favourites.

CHAPTER SEVEN

THE MENU

THE MENU

Traditional Dumplings

MAKES: 20
PREP: 35 minutes
COOK: 15 minutes

In my *Simply Chinese* cookbook I included a recipe for 'pot stickers', which are crispy, pan-fried dumplings. Boiling/poaching is one of the most popular methods for cooking dumplings, and these are called *shui gaau*. Traditionally, they are filled with pork and chive or pork and cabbage, but I use beef and cabbage here, as I think it gives a really meaty flavour (you can also use Quorn mince). My children are addicted to dumplings and they would eat them every day if I made them! Since these dumplings are boiled, they are quicker to make than the pot stickers.

INGREDIENTS

water	1 litre (34 fl oz/ 4¼ cups)
salt	

DOUGH

plain (all-purpose) flour	200 g (7 oz/1⅔ cup)
boiling water	100 ml (3½ fl oz/ scant ½ cup)
salt	¼ teaspoon
vegetable oil	½ tablespoon
cornflour (cornstarch), for dusting	

FILLING

vegetable oil	1 tablespoon
finely chopped fresh ginger root (peeled)	1 tablespoon
finely chopped garlic	1 teaspoon
napa cabbage, finely sliced	150 g (5½ oz)
light soy sauce	1 tablespoon
Shaoxing wine	1 teaspoon
white pepper	½ teaspoon
cornflour (cornstarch)	1 tablespoon
chicken stock powder	½ teaspoon
sesame oil	1 teaspoon
minced (ground) beef	200 g (7 oz)

METHOD

To make the dough, mix the flour with the boiling water and salt in a bowl until you have a rough dough that is soft to the touch but not sticky. (I wear clean rubber gloves.) (You can use a stand mixer with a dough hook or a bowl and hand-held electric whisk with dough hook attachments if you do not want to get your hands sticky, but be careful as the dough will be hot to combine).

Add the oil and work it into the dough, then leave to rest in a bowl covered with a damp dish towel or a plate for 15 minutes.

Now knead the dough by hand for 10 minutes or keep using a mixer and knead for 5 minutes. Knead until the dough is smooth – it may take another couple of minutes or more.

Cut the dough into 20 pieces and shape into flat, circular wrappers, approximately 10 cm (4 in) in diameter. You can also use a rolling pin to roll out the dough and 10 cm (4 in) cookie cutters to cut out perfect circles. Dust the wrappers with some cornflour, so they do not stick to each other.

To make the filling, heat the vegetable oil in a wok or large frying pan, then fry off the ginger and garlic for a couple of minutes. Add the napa cabbage, soy sauce and Shaoxing wine, and fry over a low heat for 5 minutes. Then mix in the remainder of the ingredients – the white pepper, cornflour, chicken stock powder, sesame oil and minced beef.

To make the dumplings, take a dough wrapper and add 1 small teaspoon of filling to the middle, then dampen the edges with some water lightly using your finger. Fold the wrapper in half to form a semi-circle. Then pull the ends of the semi-circle together so they meet and overlap slightly. Press together to join – you should now have a dumpling that looks like a tortellini.

Bring the 1 litre (34 fl oz/4¼ cups) of water to the boil in a large cooking pot with 1 teaspoon of salt.

Once the water is at a roaring boil, add half the dumplings and allow them to sink to the bottom of the pot. Bring to the boil again and allow to boil for another couple of minutes until the dumplings start floating on the

surface of the water. Remove the dumplings with a slotted spoon or spider. Then repeat the process for the rest of the dumplings.

Serve the dumplings with some black vinegar and soy sauce, just soy sauce or smothered in chilli oil – now my go-to!

- Freeze the uncooked dumplings straightaway on a baking tray, then pop into a freezer bag once frozen so they don't stick together. To cook from frozen, add a couple more minutes' boiling time.

Traditional Spring Rolls

MAKES: 12
PREP: 30 minutes (including cooling time)
COOK: 10 minutes

Spring rolls, or *chuan goon*, are eaten around Chinese New Year and are a symbol of wealth and prosperity. The appearance of the golden spring rolls is likened to gold bars and this is very auspicious. Different meats and vegetables are used in traditional recipes, but I wanted to replicate our takeaway's spring rolls as I love them. My Dad gave me the list of ingredients, but not the measurements, so this is my version. You can use store-bought wrappers or make them from scratch yourself.

INGREDIENTS

vegetable oil, for frying	

FILLING

vegetable oil	2 tablespoons
carrot, peeled and julienned	1 medium
onion, finely sliced	1
bean sprouts	200 g (7 oz)
tinned ham (such as Spam), cut into small cubes	100 g (3½ oz)
Traditional Char Siu Pork (page 59) or chicken, cubed	100 g (3½ oz)
prawns (shrimp), chopped into small pieces	100 g (3½ oz)
white pepper	½ teaspoon
pinch of salt	
pinch of sugar	
chicken stock powder	1 teaspoon
Shaoxing wine	1 tablespoon
sesame oil	1 teaspoon
five-spice powder	1 heaped teaspoon
light soy sauce	2 teaspoons

WRAPPERS

large, store-bought spring roll sheets	12, roughly 25 x 25 cm (10 x 10 in)
plain (all-purpose) flour	2 tablespoons, mixed with 4 tablespoons water to make a sealing paste

IF MAKING FROM SCRATCH

plain (all-purpose) flour	250 g (9 oz/ 2 cups)
water	375 ml (13 fl oz/ 1½ cups)
salt	½ teaspoon

TOP TIPS

- You can use leftover char siu, chicken, shiitake mushrooms or wood ear mushroom in the filling, as this is a very versatile recipe.

- Freeze the spring rolls before you fry them, then cook from frozen next time you have a craving.

- If you have any leftover wrappers, make another batch of filling for some more spring rolls, then freeze for future use.

- To save on calories, place the spring rolls on a wire rack over a baking tray, spray or brush with oil and bake in an oven preheated to 180°C fan (400°F) for about 20–25 minutes. You can even place them in the air fryer, by preheating at 200°C (400°F) and cooking between 5–8 minutes. They should be golden brown.

METHOD

To make the filling, heat the vegetable oil in a wok or large frying pan and fry off the carrot, onion and bean sprouts for a couple of minutes. Add the tinned ham, your choice of char siu or chicken, and prawns, then fry for another couple of minutes.

Add the pepper, salt, sugar, stock powder, Shaoxing wine, sesame oil, five-spice powder and light soy sauce to the wok/pan, then simmer for another 5 minutes, until all the moisture has evaporated. Remove from the heat and allow to cool to room temperature.

You now prepare the spring roll wrappers in two ways, depending on whether you are using store-bought ones or making your own.

IF USING STORE-BOUGHT WRAPPERS

Rotate the wrapper square, so one of the points is facing toward you. Then add about 4 tablespoons of the filling in a log shape, about 2.5 cm (1 in) away from the bottom point nearest to you. Fold the bottom point over the mixture into the middle, then fold first the right and then the left side over to create an envelope (make sure this is tight on the sides and at the bottom before you start rolling). Then roll tightly into a cylindrical shape up to the furthest point away from you, using your finger to seal the spring roll with some flour paste. Continue making the springs rolls in this way until all the mixture is used up.

IF MAKING THE WRAPPERS FROM SCRATCH

Mix all the wrapper ingredients together in a bowl with a whisk and then pour through a sieve and into another bowl. Put a non-stick frying pan over the lowest heat for at least 5 minutes.

Use a pastry brush to apply the wrapper mixture quickly all over the bottom of the hot, dry pan until the surface is covered. Then increase the heat for about 30 seconds until the wrapper turns white. Remove the wrapper from the pan and place between a damp cloth to stop it drying out. Wipe the pan clean with a damp cloth and repeat the process until you've used up all the wrapper mixture.

To cook the spring rolls, pour enough vegetable oil into a large saucepan, so it is double the height of the spring rolls. Heat the oil until hot. To test this, stick the handle of a wooden spoon into the oil: if bubbles start fizzing around the handle, it is hot enough to fry the spring rolls.

Carefully place three spring rolls in the pan and fry for about 2 minutes on each side until golden brown. If the spring rolls brown too quickly, reduce the heat to regulate the temperature. Cook the spring rolls in batches, placing them on some paper towel to soak up the excess oil before serving.

Chinese Daikon Cake

MAKES: 20 cm (8 in) cake or 1 kg (2 lb) loaf tin
PREP: 45 minutes
STEAM: 1 hour

Chinese daikon (mooli) cake, or *lo bak go*, is a popular dish for Chinese New Year because the word *go* is a homophone for rise/high, which obviously has an auspicious meaning, and it's also found in dim sum restaurants all year round. Many people call it Chinese turnip cake, but it is actually made from Chinese white radishes. Here, I have also used lap cheong (Chinese sausage).

INGREDIENTS

dried prawns (shrimp)	20 g (¾ oz)
large dried shiitake mushrooms	3
daikon (mooli), peeled	800 g (1 lb 12 oz)
salt	½ teaspoon
Chinese sausage (lap cheong)	1 link, approx. 50 g (1¾ oz)
vegetable oil, for frying	
garlic, grated	2 teaspoons
fresh ginger root, grated	2 teaspoons
chicken stock powder	1 tablespoon
white pepper	½ teaspoon
sugar	½ teaspoon
salt	½ teaspoon
rice flour	80 g (2¾ oz/ scant ⅔ cup)
cornflour (cornstarch)	80 g (2¾ oz/ ⅔ cup)
water	250 ml (8 fl oz/ 1 cup)

METHOD

Brush some vegetable oil over a baking tin and line with some baking parchment (the tin can be round, rectangular or square). Please note: the baking tin should fit your steamer. If using a round baking tin, it should be approx. 20 cm (8 in) in diameter or a 1 kg (2 lb) loaf tin.

Rehydrate the dried prawns in 150 ml (5 fl oz/ scant ⅔ cup) of boiling water, then set aside the soaking liquid and finely dice the prawns. Rehydrate the dried shiitake mushrooms in 200 ml (7 fl oz/scant 1 cup) of boiling water. Again, retain the soaking liquid and finely dice the mushrooms.

Grate the daikon in a food processor or use a hand grater over a bowl. Mix the salt into the grated daikon and leave for 15 minutes. Then squeeze the grated daikon through a sieve placed over another bowl to collect the liquid. There should be a lot of liquid, so pour into a measuring jug to see how much is released.

You need 250 ml (8 fl oz/1 cup) of daikon juice, but you can top this up with the soaking liquids from the shiitake mushrooms and dried prawns, so add these to the jug until you have the required amount. If there is still not enough, top up with tap water.

Blanch the Chinese sausage in a bowl of boiling water for 1 minute, then peel off the outer casing and finely dice the insides.

Heat 1 tablespoon of vegetable oil in a wok or large frying pan over a medium heat, then fry off the garlic and ginger for a couple of minutes until the aromas are released.

Add the shiitake mushrooms, prawns and sausage to the wok/pan and cook for about 5 minutes – keep stirring, as you do not want these to burn. Make sure everything is evenly coated in the ginger and garlic oil and sizzling nicely.

Remove the mushrooms, prawns and sausage from the wok/pan, and set aside. Do not clean the wok/pan.

Add the grated daikon to the same wok/pan followed by the 250 ml (8 fl oz/1 cup) of liquid you measured earlier. Bring to the boil and then stir, cooking until the daikon is translucent – this will take 5–8 minutes at most. Return the sausage, prawns and mushrooms to the wok/pan, and mix well.

Add the chicken stock powder, white pepper, sugar, salt, rice flour, cornflour and 250 ml (8 fl oz/1 cup) of water to a bowl, then whisk thoroughly before pouring into the wok/pan.

Continue stirring and cooking over a low heat until the mixture is thick and a wooden spoon run along the bottom of the wok/pan leaves a track.

Now pour the cake mixture into the prepared baking tin, ensuring it is spread out evenly and pushed into the corners.

Set up the steamer, bringing the water to a boil and then lowering to a medium simmer. Place the baking tin in the steamer and put a piece of baking parchment on top of the cake mixture to stop an accumulation of condensation. Steam the cake for an hour (you may need to add more water to the lower section of the steamer halfway through steaming). Once the cake is steamed, allow to cool and keep in the fridge.

The next day, carefully remove the cake from the baking tin and cut into slices approximately 1 cm (½ in) thick.

Pan-fry the pieces of cake in about 2 tablespoons of vegetable oil over a low heat. Fry for 3 minutes or so on each side until golden brown and do not move while each side is frying. Ensure there are gaps between the pieces in the pan to prevent them sticking to each other.

Once the pieces of cake are golden on both sides, serve with some oyster sauce, chilli oil or sriracha sauce.

TOP TIPS

- The cake freezes well because the pre-fried block or strips are easy to wrap.

- The cake can also be made with taro, which means you can use up any leftover taro from the Taro and Pork Belly recipe (page 60). You will need 300 g (10½ oz) of peeled and cubed taro, 100 g (3½ oz/generous 1 cup) glutinous rice flour and 25 g (1 oz) cornflour (cornstarch).

- You can pickle any leftover daikon: cut 350 g (12 oz) of daikon into batons and heat in a cooking pot with 100 ml (3½ fl oz/scant ½ cup) of water, 100 ml (3½ fl oz/scant ½ cup) of rice wine vinegar, 100 g (3½ oz/½ cup) of sugar and 1 teaspoon of salt until the sugar and salt have dissolved. Then pour the pickling liquid over the daikon in a sterilised glass jar and leave to sit overnight.

Char Siu Puffs

MAKES: 15
PREP: 30 minutes
COOK: 20–25 minutes

Char siu so (*so* means 'puffs') are super tasty, with the sweet char siu middle contrasting with the outer crispy, flaky pastry. These puffs are a dim sum staple and they are always fought over! I have used store-bought puff pastry because it's much more convenient.

INGREDIENTS

store-bought puff pastry	1 sheet (around 320 g/11 oz)
beaten egg, for an egg wash	1
sesame seeds, for topping	

FILLING

cooked char siu	250 g (9 oz)
light soy sauce	1 tablespoon
oyster sauce	1 tablespoon
sugar	1 teaspoon
sesame oil	1 teaspoon
red food colouring	1 teaspoon
water	150 ml (5 fl oz/ scant ⅔ cup)
cornflour (cornstarch)	1½ tablespoons

METHOD

Preheat the oven to 180°C fan (400°F) and line a baking tray (pan) with baking parchment.

To make the char siu filling, cut the char siu into small, cubed pieces. Add the remainder of the filling ingredients to a cooking pot and heat until thick – the cornflour will thicken the sauce. Then stir in the char siu and coat well. Leave the filling to cool.

To prepare the pastry, use a rolling to roll it into a rectangle, approximately 50 x 30 cm (20 x 12 in) and 2–3 mm (⅛ in) thick, between two pieces of baking parchment – this makes it easier to roll out.

Use a 10 cm (4 in) pastry cutter to cut out 15 circles, folding up and rolling out the offcuts again if you need more circles (be careful not to overwork the pastry, or it will become greasy).

Add a heaped teaspoon of the filling roughly in the shape of a triangle to the middle of each pastry circle. Brush the outer perimeter of the circles with a little water, then fold the three rounded sides into the middle and pinch all the edges together.

Flip over the puffs, so you have a smooth, triangular shape, then brush with the egg wash and sprinkle with the sesame seeds.

Place the puffs on the baking tray and bake in the oven until golden (about 20–25 minutes).

Malay Cake

MAKES: 25 cm (10 in) cake
PREP: 20 minutes to prepare; 1 hour to prove
STEAM: 30 minutes

Malay cake is also known as *Ma Lai go* in Cantonese – *Ma Lai* is 'Malay' and *go* is 'cake'. One theory on how this cake was created is that it originated in Malaysia via British influence and made its way to HK. There were no ovens traditionally back in the olden days so a steamed sponge recipe was invented. We grew up going to dim sum and fighting over this fluffy steamed cake as it was so delicious!

INGREDIENTS

evaporated milk	250 ml (8 fl oz/ 1 cup)
brown sugar, plus an extra pinch	125 g (4½ oz/ ⅔ cup)
sachet of dried active yeast	7 g (¼ oz)
vanilla extract	2 teaspoons
black treacle (molasses)	50 g (1¾ oz)
medium eggs, beaten	3 (approximately 150 g/5½ oz in weight cracked open)
vegetable oil	60 ml (2 fl oz/ ¼ cup)
plain (all-purpose) flour, sieved	200 g (7 oz/ 1⅔ cup)
cornflour (cornstarch), sieved	3 tablespoons
pinch of salt	
baking powder, sieved	1 teaspoon
bicarbonate of soda (baking soda), sieved	1 teaspoon

TOP TIPS

- The cake will keep fresh in an airtight container for a week. Reheat in the microwave covered with a damp dish cloth or steam in a bamboo steamer for 3–5 minutes, depending on the size of the piece of cake you are heating up.

- If you do not have 50 g (1¾ oz) black treacle (molasses), then use 50 g (1¾ oz/¼ cup) dark brown sugar.

METHOD

Heat the evaporated milk and a pinch of brown sugar in a large heatproof bowl for 30 seconds in the microwave or over a bain-marie until just lukewarm. Stir in the yeast, then leave to sit for 15 minutes to allow the yeast to 'bloom'.

Add the vanilla extract, treacle, 125 g (4½ oz/ ⅔ cup) of brown sugar, the eggs and vegetable oil to the bowl and mix well. Add the flour, cornflour and salt, then fold into the mixture and break up any lumps.

Let the mixture sit for another hour – this helps the batter to rest and allows the gluten to develop, so making the cake fluffy and springy when cooked.

Line a 25-cm (10-in) diameter bamboo steamer or deep cake tin (pan) with some baking parchment (you can crumple the parchment so it will fit the steamer or tin). Wrap a clean dish towel around the lid of the wok/large pot if you are not using a bamboo steamer and secure the ends with a rubber band. This will stop condensation and mottling on the cake, but ensure the towel does not touch the top of the wet batter. You can also use a large piece of baking parchment between the lid and the steamer/cake tin.

Just before steaming the cake, fold the sieved baking powder and bicarbonate of soda into the cake mixture. Then pour the mixture into the lined bamboo steamer/cake tin.

Steam over a high heat for 20–25 minutes, then reduce the heat to medium for a further 5–10 minutes – a skewer inserted into the centre of the cake will come out clean when it is ready.

Remove the cake, still inside the baking parchment lining, from the bamboo steamer/ cake tin and allow to cool on a wire rack for about 5 minutes. Once cooled, peel away the parchment and you are ready to cut the cake into pieces and serve.

Frankfurter Buns

MAKES: 8
PREP: 30 minutes to prepare; 2 hours 30 minutes to prove
COOK: APPROX. 30–40 minutes

Milk bread makes an amazing base bread dough – it is like brioche but uses a 'milk roux' paste as part of the dough. Milk bread is also the base for a huge variety of Chinese breads and one of these variations is the frankfurter bun. Mum used to go to the Chinese bakery in Belfast and get a box of baked goods, including these delicious buns. My kids fight over these when I make them.

INGREDIENTS

yeast	7 g (¼ oz)
lukewarm milk, plus extra for brushing	125 ml (4 fl oz/ ½ cup)
frankfurters	8
sesame seeds (optional) ketchup	4 tablespoons
honey	4 tablespoons

ROUX

plain (all-purpose) flour	3 tablespoons
milk	65 ml (2 fl oz/ ¼ cup)
water	55 ml (1¾ fl oz/ 3½ tablespoons)

DOUGH

plain (all-purpose) flour	350 g (12 oz/ 2¾ cups)
sugar	35 g (1¼ oz/ 3 tablespoons)
condensed milk	40 g (1½ oz)
salt	3 g
medium egg	1
butter, melted	60 g (2 oz)

SUGAR SYRUP

caster (superfine) sugar	50 g (1¾ oz/ ¼ cup)
boiling water	50 ml (1¾ fl oz/ 3½ tablespoons)

METHOD

Add the yeast to the lukewarm milk. The yeast will 'bloom' in the milk, which speeds up the proving process.

To make the roux, mix all the ingredients in a cup to make a paste, then warm in the microwave for 2 x 30 second bursts and stir or cook in a small saucepan on the stove-top on a low heat until it has thickened (3–5 minutes) – keep stirring.

To make the dough, mix the roux, flour, sugar, condensed milk, salt, egg and the yeast mixture in a stand mixer with a dough hook, or use a bowl and hand-held electric whisk with dough hook attachments, for 3–5 minutes until combined. Add the melted butter while the mixer/electric whisk is still running and mix until completely incorporated. You can also knead in manually to combine.

Leave the dough to sit for 20 minutes covered with a damp dish towel. Return the dough to the mixer/bowl and mix for 5 minutes at medium speed.

Shape the dough into a ball by tucking under until the surface is nice and smooth. Return the dough to the mixer/bowl and leave covered for approx. 1 hour–1 hour 30 minutes until it has doubled in size. A quick method is to put the dough in the oven with the light on, which will be warm enough to prove the dough.

Preheat the oven to 180°C fan (400°F) and line a large baking tin with baking parchment.

Remove the dough from the mixer/bowl, then punch down the dough and divide it into 8 portions. Roll each portion into a log shape (with the middle part thicker than the ends) and wrap this around a frankfurter.

Cover the rolls once more and leave for 45 minutes–1 hour to double in size, again putting them in the oven with the light on.

Brush the tops of the rolls with some milk, being careful not to let it drip down the sides too much, otherwise the rolls will stick to the tin. Top the rolls with a sprinkling of sesame seeds (if using).

Bake the rolls on the bottom shelf of the oven until golden brown (about 30–40 minutes).

While the rolls are baking, make a sugar syrup by dissolving the sugar in the water and allowing to cool.

As soon as you remove the rolls from the oven, brush all over immediately with the sugar syrup. Serve with the ketchup and honey mixed together.

TOP TIPS

- Letting the dough sit (a process known as autolysing) helps to develop the gluten and also makes it easier to knead if you do not have a stand mixer.

- Any leftover frankfurters can be made into octopus frankfurters for the Crispy Chilli Egg Noodle Bowl recipe (page 92).

Lava Custard Buns

MAKES: 12
PREP: 30 minutes to prepare; 1 hour to prove
STEAM: 12–15 minutes

Lava buns are so tasty and they also deliver on their name ... if you eat them too quickly when they have just been steamed, the filling really is like molten lava! No one wants to have a burned tongue. Using salted egg yolks gives the buns that sweet-salty combo like a salted caramel, which everyone loves now. If you don't have salted egg yolks, then just use normal egg yolks and add a pinch of sea salt.

INGREDIENTS

BAO DOUGH (APPROX. 12 X 40 G/1½ OZ PIECES)

sachet of dried active yeast	7 g (¼ oz)
sugar	2 tablespoons
milk	100 ml (3½ fl oz/ scant ½ cup)
warm water	100 ml (3½ fl oz/ scant ½ cup)
plain (all-purpose) flour	300 g (10½ oz/ 2½ cups)
cornflour (cornstarch)	75 g (2½ oz/ ⅔ cup)
salt	2 g
vegetable oil	1 tablespoon

EGG YOLK FILLING (APPROX. 12 X 25 G/1 OZ PIECES)

salted egg yolks, steamed (page 46)	3
softened butter	50 g (1¾ oz)
icing (powdered) sugar, sieved	60 g (2 oz/½ cup)
custard powder, sieved	30 g (1 oz/¼ cup)
milk powder	50 g (1¾ oz/½cup)
milk	1 tablespoon
vanilla extract	1 teaspoon

TOP TIP

- Freeze the lava buns and cook them from frozen, adding an extra 5 minutes to the steaming time to ensure the insides are fully heated through (remember to wait 5 minutes before biting into one).

METHOD

To make the filling, separate the salted egg yolks from the whites. Put the egg yolks in a bowl, set up a steamer and then steam for 20 minutes. The yolks will turn bright yellow/orange. Remove the yolks from the bowl and smash with the flat side of a large kitchen knife blade, then use the knife to cut the yolks into uneven pieces until they resemble a paste or fine crumbs. Then add the butter, icing sugar, custard powder, milk powder, milk and vanilla extract to the bowl and mix until everything is well combined and forms a thick dough.

Divide the yolk filling into roughly twelve – approx. 25 g (1 oz) pieces – and roll into balls. Keep the balls in the fridge for at least 15 minutes to firm up. You can also make the balls the night before and keep covered in the fridge.

To make the bao dough, mix the yeast, sugar, milk and warm water in a stand mixer, or use a bowl and hand-held electric whisk, and allow to 'bloom' for 15 minutes. The surface should be all bubbly.

Add the flour, cornflour, salt and oil to the mixer/bowl, then knead the dough with the mixer's dough hook or use the electric whisk with dough hook attachments for 5 minutes. If the dough is dry, add another splash of water.

Leave the dough to sit for 20 minutes covered with a damp dish towel. Return the dough to the mixer/bowl and mix for 5 minutes at medium speed.

Shape the dough into a ball by tucking under until the surface is nice and smooth. Return the dough to the mixer/bowl and leave covered until it has doubled in size – this can take up to an hour. A quick method is to put the dough in the oven with the light on, which will be warm enough to prove the dough.

Punch down the dough and divide into twelve – approx. 50 g (1¾ oz) portions. Roll the dough portions into balls, then flatten with a rolling pin into circles about 12 cm (5 in) in diameter.

Hold a dough circle in the palm of one hand, then add a yolk filling to the middle and tuck the edges of the dough around the filling. Nip the excess dough closed at the top,

so there are no gaps, making sure the dough is wrapped tightly around the filling. When you turn the bun the right way up, the top surface should be nice and smooth. Repeat for all the dough circles and yolk fillings.

Place the buns, crease side down, on a square of baking parchment in the fridge or 10 minutes to firm up.

While the buns are firming up, set up a steamer. Bring the water in the lower section to a boil, then lower to a simmer, place the buns in the steaming section and steam for 12–15 minutes. Place a piece of baking parchment over the buns, so condensation does not ruin the surface.

Remove the buns from the steamer and allow to cool for 5 minutes before serving – they really are like molten lava unless you are careful!

Mantou Buns

MAKES: 12
PREP: 1 hour to prepare; 1 hour to prove
STEAM: 15 minutes

Mantou buns are steamed plain bao buns with no filling and they are popular in northern China. My Mum used to deep-fry these steamed buns and allow us to dip them in condensed milk! I've discovered this is another dish that is served at dim sum restaurants in Hong Kong and sometimes you can get them steamed along with the deep-fried versions – and always with a big helping of condensed milk.

INGREDIENTS

vegetable oil, for deep-frying and brushing	
condensed milk, to serve	

BAO DOUGH (APPROX. 12 X 50 G/1¾ OZ PIECES)

sachet of dried active yeast	7 g (¼ oz)
sugar	2 tablespoons
warm water	200 ml (7 fl oz/ scant 1 cup)
plain (all-purpose) flour	300 g (10½ oz/ 2½ cups)
cornflour (cornstarch)	75 g (2½ oz/ ⅔ cup)
salt	2 g
vegetable oil	1 tablespoon

TOP TIPS

- You can freeze the cooked mantou buns for up to a month and then cook them from frozen. Just add an extra 2–3 minutes to the steaming time to ensure the insides are heated through.

- Instead of deep-frying, brush cold steamed buns with a little oil, then cook in an air fryer for 5 minutes – they will be super crisp and golden.

METHOD

To make the bao dough, mix the yeast, sugar and water in a stand mixer, or use a mixing bowl and hand-held electric whisk, and allow to 'bloom' for 15 minutes. The surface should be all bubbly.

Add the flour, cornflour, salt and vegetable oil to the mixer/bowl, then knead the dough for 5 minutes with either the mixer's dough hook or the electric whisk in the bowl with dough hook attachments.

Leave the dough to sit for 20 minutes covered with a damp dish towel. Return the dough to the mixer/bowl and mix for 5 minutes at medium speed.

Shape the dough into a ball by tucking under until the surface is nice and smooth. Return the dough to the mixer/bowl and leave covered until it has doubled in size – this can take up to an hour. A quick method is to put the dough in the oven with the light on, which will be warm enough to prove the dough.

Punch down the dough and divide into two equal balls. Roll each ball with a rolling pin into a flat square measuring 20 x 20 cm (8 x 8 in). Brush the dough squares with a very thin layer of water and roll tightly so there are no air pockets.

Using a super-sharp knife, remove the tails from the logs of dough and divide each log into 6 even buns, so you have 12 buns in total. Put the buns on a square of baking parchment and allow to rest for about 10 minutes.

While the buns are resting, set up a steamer, bringing the water to a boil and then lowering to a simmer. Add the buns to the steamer (ensuring there is at least a 2.5 cm/1 in gap between each bun).

Brush the buns with a thin layer of oil and steam for 10–12 minutes – place a piece of baking parchment over the buns so condensation does not ruin the surface.

You can eat the buns steamed, but to make the delicious, deep-fried version, heat 5 cm (2 in) of vegetable oil in a wok or cooking pot until hot – the handle of a wooden spoon should fizz when the oil is hot enough.

Fry the buns for a couple of minutes on each side until golden.

Remove the buns from the wok/pot with a slotted spoon and place on some paper towel to soak up excess oil. Fry as many buns as you like, but do not overcrowd the wok/pot.

Serve the buns with lashings of condensed milk.

DESSERTS

08 八

甜品

I love a sweet treat and writing a cookbook without a section on desserts for me would be absurd! I have gathered together a few recipes here that I enjoy myself. Some of them evoked very old memories and had me craving them when I started writing up the recipes. It's funny how food can transport you to different times in your life and you can really develop a great attachment to various dishes.

CHAPTER EIGHT

THE MENU

**GLUTINOUS
RICE BALLS**
146

**STEAMED
EGG PUDDING**
149

**CHESTNUT
TARTLETS**
150

**NO-CHURN
BLACK SESAME
ICE CREAM**
152

THE MENU

**MUM'S SPECIAL
FRUIT SALAD**
155

**FLUFFY BIRTHDAY
CUPCAKES**
156

Glutinous Rice Balls

MAKES: 15 balls
PREP: 30 minutes
COOK: 10 minutes

These rice balls, or *tong yuan*, are a truly celebratory dish and made for big celebrations and festivals. The words are homophonic with 'union' and therefore symbolise success and togetherness. The balls are traditionally eaten at the Lantern Festival during Chinese New Year and to mark other auspicious times such as weddings and the night before a wedding at the 'hair combing' ceremony. I enjoyed this ceremony at my own wedding, and although it is usually carried out by the mother of the bride, I was honoured when my Auntie Linda stepped in and performed the ritual for me. Traditionally, they are simply plain, poached glutinous rice balls without any filling in a sweet ginger syrup. This recipe is for rice balls filled with peanut butter and served with a sugar syrup – my favourite.

INGREDIENTS

FILLING

crunchy peanut butter	2 heaped tablespoons
granulated sugar	1 tablespoon
salted peanuts, roughly chopped	2 tablespoons

SUGAR SYRUP

water	750 ml (25 fl oz/ 3 cups)
brown sugar	75 g (2½ oz/ scant ½ cup)

DOUGH

glutinous rice flour, plus extra if needed	130 g (4½ oz/ 1 cup)
icing (powdered) sugar, sieved	1 tablespoon
boiling water, plus extra if needed	60 ml (2 fl oz/ ¼ cup)

METHOD

To prepare the filling, mix the peanut butter, granulated sugar and salted peanuts in a bowl.

Keep in the fridge to firm up for at least 15 minutes, then shape just over ½ teaspoon of filling into a ball shape (approx. 15 balls of filling). Repeat until all the filling mixture is used up. Put the balls on a plate and keep in the freezer until needed (about another 15 minutes), otherwise the mixture will be hard to work with.

While the filling is chilling in the fridge, make the sugar syrup. Add the water and sugar to a cooking pot and bring to a simmer for a couple of minutes until the sugar has dissolved.

Next make the dough. Add the flour and icing sugar to a mixing bowl, slowly pour in half the boiling water and mix in quickly with a wooden spoon. Then add the rest of the water and keep mixing.

Once the dough is cool enough to handle with your hands (but still hot), turn out onto a work surface and knead for a couple of minutes. If the dough is dry and cracking, add a couple of drops of water; if it is too sticky, add a little more flour. You are looking for a smooth, stretchy dough.

Now divide the dough into 15 balls. The easiest way to do this is to roll the piece of dough into a log, then use a sharp knife to cut it into equal portions. You then roll each portion into a ball and put on a plate. When working each dough ball, cover the rest with a damp dish towel to stop them drying out.

Hold each dough ball in the palm of one hand, then make an indentation in the middle with a finger of your other hand large enough to hold the filling.

Remove the filling from the freezer and work quickly. Press a ball of filling into the indentation in each of the dough balls. Then gather the sides of each dough ball upwards and enclose the filling.

Roll the filled dough balls between your hands, checking for cracks. Keep rolling until all the cracks have disappeared. Once you have rolled each ball smooth, return to the plate and keep covered with the damp dish towel until you have rolled all the balls.

Bring a litre (34 fl oz/4¼ cups) of water to a roaring boil in a cooking pot, then add half of the filled balls at a time. Let the balls float, then allow to boil for a further minute. Remove the balls from the pot with a slotted spoon and place in a bowl of cold tap water (to stop them sticking to each other). Repeat for the remainder of the balls.

To serve, place three balls in a bowl and pour over the sugar syrup to just cover them. You can have more balls per portion, but I find three is my limit at any one time.

TOP TIPS

- Freeze the fully formed tong yuan before you boil them. Ideal when you have a sweet craving.

- Tong yuan are the hot version of the ever-popular *mochi*. If you would like to make the cold version (with the same ingredients), instead of boiling the water, use cold water in a microwavable bowl. Cover the bowl and heat in the microwave for 1 minute, mix and microwave for another minute, and then mix again. You should have a thick, shiny dough. Roll out the dough with some cornflour (cornstarch) sprinkled over the work surface, then use 8 cm (3 in) cookie cutters to cut it into circles. Wrap the circles of dough around the filling, cover with cling film (plastic wrap) and chill in the fridge or freezer, depending on your choice of filling – you could use the No-Churn Black Sesame Ice Cream (page 152), for example.

Steamed Egg Pudding

MAKES: 4
PREP: 10 minutes
STEAM: 15 minutes

I loved it when Mum made these egg puddings – they were never really planned because it is such an easy recipe made with only four ingredients that she could just rustle them up and pop them in the steamer. They are like a smooth set custard with a crème brûlée flavour.

INGREDIENTS

water	250 ml (8 fl oz/ 1 cup)
evaporated milk	300 g (10½ oz)
eggs, beaten	4
caster (superfine) sugar	8 teaspoons

METHOD

Put a bowl or large measuring jug on top of a set of digital scales and measure out the water, evaporated milk, eggs and sugar, then whisk to combine.

Set up a steamer, bringing the water to a boil and then lowering to a simmer. Put the ramekins in the steamer and pour the egg liquid directly through a sieve into each one. Sieving the liquid removes any air bubbles and lumps from the liquid.

Tightly cover each ramekin in the steamer with some cling film (plastic wrap). I usually wear rubber gloves to do this, so I am not scalded. Alternatively, lift off the top steamer section from the pot where the puddings are in and lift off the lid (so you are not in direct line of steam) and cover the ramekins away from the steam.

Steam the filled ramekins for 10 minutes. To check whether the puddings are set, do the jiggle test, by shaking them gently. The middles should have a slight jiggle to them. They may need another couple of minutes to firm up. Then remove from the heat.

Be careful when you remove the cling film to avoid leaving marks on the puddings. It's fine if a little water splatters over them, as it doesn't affect the taste at all. Enjoy hot or cold.

TOP TIP

- The puddings can be reheated in the steamer or given a quick 1–2-minute burst in the microwave to heat through.

Chestnut Tartlets

MAKES: 10
PREP: 10 minutes
COOK: 25 minutes

Chestnuts add a lovely texture and sweetness to all dishes. I have fond memories of going to the bakery in Hong Kong with Mum and getting decadent chestnut purée cakes and tarts. I have changed this to a low-key version using just three simple ingredients to create a delicious filling.

INGREDIENTS

PASTRY

store-bought shortcrust pastry	250 g (9 oz)

FILLING

cooked peeled chestnuts (vacuum-packed chestnuts)	180 g (6½ oz)
dark brown sugar	2 tablespoons
vanilla extract	1 teaspoon
boiling water	150 ml (5 fl oz/ scant ⅔ cup)

TOPPING

whipping cream	200 ml (7 fl oz/ scant 1 cup)
condensed milk	4 tablespoons

TOP TIPS

- When blind baking the pastry cases, cut squares of baking parchment about 4 cm (1½ in) larger than the diameter of the bun tin indentations. Crumple each piece of paper to fit the indentations and add the ceramic baking beans – the paper will fit more tightly and snugly to the pastry, so the weight of the baking beans keeps the pastry flat.

- This dessert is ideal if you have any chestnuts left over from making the Chicken and Chestnuts recipe (page 49).

METHOD

Preheat the oven to 180°C fan (400°F).

To prepare the pastry bases for the tartlets, roll out the pastry with a rolling pin between two pieces of baking parchment until 2–3 mm (⅛ in) thick. Then use a 9–10 cm (3½–4 in) cookie cutter to cut out 10 circles and place them in a non-stick bun tin (pan).

Place a small piece of baking parchment on top of each pastry case and add a few ceramic baking beans (you can also use uncooked rice or lentils) to weight it down (see Top Tips below, for more advice). Blind bake the pastry cases in the oven for 15 minutes, then take out and carefully remove the baking parchment and beans/rice/lentils.

Return the pastry cases to the oven, uncovered, for 10 minutes to crisp up, then remove and allow to cool.

To make the filling, place the chestnuts in a cooking pot, add the sugar, vanilla and water, then slowly bring up to a boil and simmer for 15 minutes. This should soften the chestnuts.

Remove the pot from the heat, then use a hand blender to blitz the chestnuts into a purée until smooth. If the paste is too runny, then heat for longer – you are looking for a whipped consistency. Leave to cool.

To make the topping, whip the cream with the condensed milk to stiff peaks and then put in a piping bag.

To assemble the tarts, add a dollop of sweet, smooth chestnut purée to each pastry shell, spread over the bottom and then pipe over the cream.

No-Churn Black Sesame Ice Cream

MAKES: 1 x 1 kg (2 lb) plastic container
PREP: 20 minutes
FREEZING: 6 hours

During lockdown I made this no-churn ice cream with just cream and condensed milk, and it was a real hit! Here I have taken it to another level by including a different flavour. Black sesame seeds are an extremely popular ingredient with a wonderful flavour, which is even more intense and fragrant when the seeds are toasted. You can make a delightfully creamy ice cream from only four ingredients – it's a must-try.

INGREDIENTS

black sesame seeds	150 g (5½ oz/ 1 cup)
whipping cream	600 ml (20 fl oz/ 2½ cups)
condensed milk	1 tin (approx. 397 g/14 oz)
vanilla extract	1 teaspoon

METHOD

Toast the sesame seeds in a hot, dry pan until sizzling and then blitz in a spice grinder or coffee bean grinder, or use a mortar and pestle (for about 5 minutes). There will be a lovely aroma!

To make the ice cream, whisk the cream to soft peaks in a bowl and then whisk in the condensed milk and vanilla extract – be careful not to curdle the cream at this stage. You are looking for soft peaks (*not* stiff peaks).

Pour half of the mixture into an airtight plastic container, then toss the blitzed sesame seeds in and, using a knife, lightly swirl through the layer of ice cream. Repeat by adding in the rest of the ice cream and tossing in the remaining black sesame paste, then lightly swirl through the top of the ice cream. Spread right into the corners. Pop in the freezer for at least 6 hours.

Once you have opened the container, place a piece of cling film (plastic wrap) neatly on top of the ice cream (ensure it touches the surface) to stop it crystallising.

TOP TIPS

- This is an ideal dessert because it can be made days in advance.

Mum's Special Fruit Salad

SERVES: 4–6
PREP: 20 minutes
COOK: 10 minutes

I scoured books and the internet trying to find the origins of this recipe, but to no avail. My Mum used to serve this fruit salad at all big family gatherings and birthday parties – I have asked my siblings and they all have really lovely memories of it. However, it contains some unconventional ingredients for a fruit salad, such as potatoes, eggs and evaporated milk. I consider it to be more like a Waldorf salad.

INGREDIENTS

eggs	2
medium potato, peeled and cut into 1.5 cm (½ in) cubes	1 (approx. 150 g/5½ oz)
eating (dessert) apples of your choice (I like Granny Smith in this salad, but Mum used Red Delicious), cored and chopped into rough chunks	2
cocktail fruit, drained	1 tin (415 g/ 14½ oz)

SALAD DRESSING

salad cream	100 g (3½ oz)
evaporated milk	40 g (1½ oz)
pinch of salt	

METHOD

Bring some water to a roaring boil in a saucepan. Once boiling, place in the eggs and cook for 8 minutes, so that they are hard-boiled. Allow to cool, then peel off the shells, dice and set aside.

Put the potato cubes in a cooking pot of cold water and bring to a boil and cook for 10 minutes until the potato is cooked. Set aside.

To make the salad dressing, put a bowl on top of some digital scales, weigh out the salad cream and evaporated milk, add the pinch of salt, and mix to combine.

Add your choice of apples and the tinned fruit to the bowl and mix well. Finally, add the potatoes and eggs and toss through the dressing.

Keep the fruit salad covered in the fridge until you are ready to serve.

TOP TIP

- You can adjust the taste of the dressing and use the ingredients in different proportions. I like a sharper dressing, so I added an extra squeeze of salad cream. Taste and see what you prefer.

Fluffy Birthday Cupcakes

MAKES: 12
PREP: 15 minutes
COOK: 45 minutes

Chinese birthday cakes are chiffon-based cakes topped with lots of cream and fresh fruit. However, they take a lot of time to prepare and the chiffon cake has to rest upside down in the cake tin (pan) until fully cooled. Otherwise the lovely, light air pockets will be compressed if the cake is flipped over straightaway. So here is a simple, fluffy, no-fuss recipe for the same cake, but as individual cupcakes.

INGREDIENTS

BATTER

milk	50 ml (1¾ fl oz/ 3½ tablespoons)
vegetable oil	2 tablespoons
egg yolks	3 medium
vanilla extract	2 teaspoons
plain (all-purpose) flour, sieved	75 g (2½ oz/ ½ cup)

MERINGUE

egg whites	3 medium
fresh lemon juice	1 teaspoon
caster (superfine) sugar	50 g (1¾ oz/ ¼ cup)
cornflour (cornstarch), sieved	1 tablespoon

TOPPING

whipping cream	200 ml (7 fl oz/ scant 1 cup)
icing (powdered) sugar, sieved	2 tablespoons
vanilla extract	2 teaspoons
assortment of sliced fresh fruit, such as blueberries, raspberries, strawberries and kiwi	

METHOD

Preheat the oven to 150°C fan (350°F). Line a 12-hole muffin tin (pan) with baking parchment cut into 20 x 20 cm (8 x 8 in) squares. You can also use deep muffin cases to line the tin.

To make the batter, whisk the milk and oil together in a bowl until well combined. Add the egg yolks and vanilla extract, then the sieved flour and keep whisking. The mixture should resemble a thick, pale yellow batter.

To make the meringue, put the egg whites in a clean, grease-free bowl with the lemon juice and whisk to soft peaks. Add the sugar in thirds, whisking to soft peaks after each addition. The whisked egg whites should be glossy and stiff. At this point, add the sieved cornflour and fold in – you want a mallow-like texture.

Now add 4 tablespoons of the meringue to the batter to loosen it, then carefully fold the batter into the meringue until well combined (the batter should be the same colour throughout with no streaks).

Divide the batter between the 12 cases in the muffin tin and bake in the oven on the middle shelf for 45 minutes. The cupcakes are ready when a skewer inserted into the middle comes out clean. Remove from the oven and leave to cool.

While the cupcakes are cooling, whip the cream with the icing sugar and vanilla extract until you have firm peaks, then spread over the cupcakes and top with your choice of fruit.

TOP TIP

• Only decorate the cupcakes when you know you will be eating within a two-hour period (otherwise the cream will make the sponge soggy).

DRINKS

09 九

饮料

For this chapter I have put together a number of my favourite drinks, which are popular in all the eating establishments in Hong Kong. Drinks such as Horlicks and Ovaltine are served hot or cold, while yuan yeung cha (tea and coffee mixed together, then finished with evaporated milk and sweetened with condensed milk) is a strangely addictive drink. The sought-after cream soda with milk drink was a birthday party classic in my family (we were only allowed fizzy drinks on special occasions).

CHAPTER NINE

THE MENU

HOMEMADE
SOY MILK
160

TEA/COFFEE
162

CREAM SODA
AND MILK
165

HORLICKS
AND OVALTINE
166

BUBBLE TEA
168

饮 料 饮 料

Homemade Soy Milk

MAKES: 6 glasses (approx. 250 ml/8 fl oz)
SOAKING TIME: 8–12 hours or overnight
PREP: 30 minutes

Mum used to make soy milk from scratch all the time and then she turned it into a silky-smooth soy milk steamed pudding. Both the drink and the pudding are popular in the street markets (*dai pai dong*) and dim sum restaurants in Hong Kong.

INGREDIENTS

raw dried soy beans	250 g (9 oz)
water	2 litres (68 fl oz/ 8½ cups)
brown or white sugar, to sweeten	2 tablespoons

METHOD

Soak the soy beans in 750 ml (25 fl oz/3 cups) of cold water in a bowl for 8–12 hours or overnight.

Rinse and remove the skins from the soy beans by rubbing them together in your hands. Rinse and rub away as much of the skins as you can.

Then blitz the soybeans in two batches in a blender/or hand-held blender and a jug – adding 1 litre (34 fl oz/4¼ cups) of water to each batch to make into a smooth thick mixture (there will be tiny lumps visible).

Put the strained soy milk in a large cooking pot.

Bring to the boil and cook for a couple of minutes, then reduce to a low simmer with the lid of the pot on. Foam will form on top, so scoop this off as much as you can.

Keep stirring the soy milk until it no longer has a very earthy/raw smell and taste. The longer you cook the milk, the more intense the soy flavour becomes. Turn off the heat and allow to cool. If you have time, strain the milk again through a clean washed muslin cloth (cheesecloth) to make sure there are definitely no lumps of blitzed soy beans.

Taste and adjust to your liking, adding brown or white sugar to sweeten. For this quantity of soy milk, I would start with a tablespoon of sugar first, then taste and add more if necessary.

TOP TIPS

- Leftover soy milk can be made into tofu by adding lemon juice. It is just like making cheese with milk and is super simple – check out my recipe for Homemade Tofu on page 111.

- You can also make a tasty soy milk pudding by adding gelatine powder to the basic soy milk. Take 350 ml (12 fl oz/1½ cups) of warmed soy milk and add 1 teaspoon of gelatine (dissolved in 2 tablespoons of warm soy milk). Mix together, pour into two bowls and allow to set in the fridge for about 4 hours. Serve hot or cold and with a sugar or ginger syrup.

Tea/Coffee

MAKES: 2 mugs
PREP: 15 minutes

This marriage of two of my favourite caffeinated drinks originated in Hong Kong and is ever popular in the street markets and *cha chaan teng* restaurants. It was supposedly invented in the 1950s, and the balance of the drink should be 7 parts milk tea and 3 parts coffee. This recipe has a strong coffee flavour, which I think complements the tea and the sweetness of the condensed milk. You can also use sugar to sweeten the drink if you do not like condensed milk.

INGREDIENTS

tea bags (of strong black tea)	2
water	500 ml (17 fl oz/ generous 2 cups)
instant coffee granules	4 teaspoons
condensed milk	2 tablespoons
evaporated milk	4 tablespoons

METHOD

Bring the two tea bags to the boil with the water in a saucepan, then simmer for 10 minutes. Add the instant coffee granules, condensed milk and evaporated milk.

Remove the tea bags, then pour the drink into two mugs, or you can pour over ice once the tea/coffee has cooled down.

TOP TIPS

- Play around with the balance of the flavour! You can add less or more of the tea or coffee and same for the milkiness.

Cream Soda and Milk

MAKES: 568 ml (1 pint)
PREP: 5 minutes

This was a major treat at birthday parties when we were young as Mum didn't allow us to have fizzy drinks. But at parties or big meals at our house we were allowed cream soda! I have no idea where adding milk came from, but it is reminiscent of an ice cream float and is a popular drink in Hong Kong.

INGREDIENTS

cold milk	approx. 250 ml (8 fl oz/1 cup)
chilled cream soda	1 can (330 ml/ 11¼ fl oz/ 1⅓ cups)
ice cubes	

METHOD

Pour the milk into the bottom of a pint glass, then pour in the cream soda. This will create a creamy, bubbly top. Add ice and enjoy.

Horlicks and Ovaltine

MAKES: 1 mug
PREP: 5 minutes

Horlicks and Ovaltine were my favourite hot childhood drinks. I just loved their malty flavour and I even remember Mum buying us the Horlicks and Ovaltine 'sweets/tablets'. When I went to Hong Kong for the first time I was surprised to find the drinks were served everywhere; their popularity was due to the Commonwealth Charter that promoted the exchange of cultural ideas, which resulted in these products making their way to Hong Kong.

Served in Hong Kong's cha chaan teng restaurants, these malted drinks hold deep childhood memories for me. Ovaltine and Horlicks powders were kept in huge containers in the kitchen, then made up freshly with boiling water and finished with some milk as per the instructions. You were also given sugar sachets for sweetening if you wished. Both drinks can be served hot or cold!

METHOD

Stir Horlicks or Ovaltine powder into the boiling water. Then top with the hot milk.

Taste and sweeten according to preference with sugar or some condensed milk.

INGREDIENTS

Horlicks or Ovaltine powder	30 g (1 oz/5 heaped teaspoons)
boiling water	50 ml (1¾ fl oz/3½ tablespoons)
hot milk	200 ml (7 fl oz/scant 1 cup)
sugar or condensed milk	to taste
evaporated milk	

Bubble Tea

MAKES: 568 ml (1 pint)
PREP: 15 minutes

Hong Kong had bubble tea for decades before it became a craze around five years ago, so it makes me chuckle as I have known about it since I was teeny tiny going to Hong Kong on holidays. We drank lots of different versions of bubble tea.

INGREDIENTS

water	250 ml (8 fl oz/ 1 cup)
tapioca pearls	4 tablespoons
soft brown sugar	2 tablespoons
brewed black tea, cooled	250 ml (8 fl oz/ 1 cup)
evaporated milk	1 tablespoon
ice cubes	

METHOD

Pour the water into a small cooking pot and bring to the boil, then add the tapioca pearls. Remove the pearls when they start floating (after about 5 minutes).

Add the tapioca pearls to the bottom of a serving glass, then add the sugar and mix. Next pour the cooled brewed tea into the glass, along with the evaporated milk and a handful of ice cubes.

Taste the bubble tea and add more sugar or milk to your liking. Make sure you have a wide enough straw to suck up the tapioca pearls, otherwise enjoy eating them with a spoon!

ABOUT THE AUTHOR

Suzie Lee is a Chinese cook, the 2020 winner of *BBC's Best Home Cook* and the presenter of *Suzie Lee: Home Cook Hero*. Brought up by her Hong Kong parents in Northern Ireland, Suzie was taught to cook by her mum Celia, who sadly passed away when she was just 16. Even before winning *Best Home Cook*, Suzie was always being asked for her recipes and top tips in the kitchen. Suzie gives demonstrations at a range of regional and national food shows around the UK and has worked with a leading supermarket in Northern Ireland to develop a range of brand-new ready meals.

ACKNOWLEDGEMENTS

This is my second cookbook and if you have come across my first book, you will know *Simply Chinese* is inspired by my Mum, who unfortunately is no longer with us. My Mum has been my inspiration in all areas of life and, most importantly, my love of food; she is the woman who gave me my grit and determination to do my very best in whatever I was doing.

Simply Chinese Feasts is the essence of Chinese cuisine – sharing. It does not need to be a special occasion to have a feast – it is about food you can enjoy with friends and family! Thank you, Mum, this book is for you, as you made me appreciate the importance of food for any occasion.

Stevie, my hubby, who is the calm one in our relationship – I am the hyper and mad one! He pushed and supported me when I had a massive speed wobble during writing this book as I destroyed my laptop... Hot honey and lemon tea got spilt over my keyboard... don't even ask... I still can't talk about it!

My two babies (ok, they aren't so wee anymore), Zander and Odie, for being tough critics but trying everything I put in front of them. Getting their honest opinions made me rethink and therefore modify some of my recipes to cut down time and make dishes simpler to cook.

My siblings, Angela, Winnie, Veronica, Timmy, and Dad, who all had their input into this book.

My top food testers, Jonny Baxter, Jill Caskey and Rachel Scott, your honest opinions were very welcomed.

Anne Kibel, my lovely agent who always believes in me even when I don't! She saw the importance of me wanting to explore my food heritage and this second book has allowed me to delve further into Chinese festivals and food linked with them.

Lynne and Ivan Arbuthnot (my in-laws), Elizabeth Ramsey, Rachel and Matt Fraser, who have been my support network throughout this writing process. I am indebted to them for all the school pick-ups and drop-offs when I have been writing these recipes. Thank you from the bottom of my heart!

Kate Burkett and Eila Purvis from HG, thank you for having the confidence in me and for publishing this cookbook. Lizzie Mayson, Kitty Coles, Clare Cole and the team at Evi-O. Studio for making it all come together; the book is just stunning. Thank you!

INDEX

R

rice
 glutinous rice balls 146–7
 'no claypot' rice 94–5
 the perfect boiled rice 100
 quick congee 91
 salmon fried rice 86
 yung chow fried rice 96

S

salads
 spicy cucumber salad 105
salmon fried rice 86
salted chicken eggs 46–7
salted chilli chicken 44–5
satay sauce
 mixed vegetable satay 106
sausages
 Chinese daikon cake 132–3
 'no claypot' rice 94–5
scallops with mushrooms and pak choi 31
sea bream
 crispy sea bream 20
seafood
 fish ball noodle soup 26–7
 hot pot 78
 king prawn eggs 28
 lobster noodles 22–4
 scallops with mushrooms and pak choi 31
sesame seeds
 mum's crunchy sesame seed chicken 38
 no-churn black sesame ice cream 152
 spicy chilli oil 122
shredded chicken and choot choi noodles 88
soup
 ABC soup 75
 chicken and watercress soup 70
 drunken chicken soup 80
 fish ball noodle soup 26–7
 hot pot 78
 pork and lotus root soup 72
 spinach egg drop soup 76
soy beans
 homemade soy milk 160
soy milk
 homemade soy milk 160
 homemade tofu 111
spinach egg drop soup 76
spring rolls
 traditional spring rolls 128–9
steaming 17
stir-fries 17
 mixed vegetable and crispy tofu stir-fry 114
 spicy lotus root stir-fry 116
sweetcorn 106
 ABC soup 75
 chicken, sweetcorn and carrot 42

T

takeaways 13
tapioca
 bubble tea 168
taro and pork belly 60–1
tea 162
 bubble tea 168
tofu
 crispy chilli egg noodle bowl 92
 homemade tofu 111
 hot pot 78
 mixed vegetable and crispy tofu stir-fry 114
 quick congee 91
 spinach egg drop soup 76
 steamed silken tofu 120
tomatoes
 ABC soup 75
traditional char siu pork 59

V

vegetables
 crispy chilli egg noodle bowl 92
 hot pot 78
 mixed vegetable and crispy tofu stir-fry 114
 mixed vegetable satay 106
vinegar
 pork belly in black vinegar 56

W

water chestnuts
 Kung Po chicken 50–1
watercress
 chicken and watercress soup 70
weddings 9
white cut chicken 52
woks 16

Y

yung chow fried rice 96

Published in 2024 by Hardie Grant Books,
an imprint of Hardie Grant Publishing

Hardie Grant Books (London)
5th & 6th Floors
52–54 Southwark Street
London SE1 1UN

Hardie Grant Books (Melbourne)
Building 1, 658 Church Street
Richmond, Victoria 3121

hardiegrantbooks.com

Text © Suzie Lee
Photography © Lizzie Mayson
Illustrations © Evi-O. Studio

British Library Cataloguing-in-Publication Data.
A catalogue record for this book is available
from the British Library.

Simply Chinese Feasts

ISBN: 978-1-78488-676-9

10 9 8 7 6 5 4 3 2 1

Publishing Director: Kajal Mistry
Commissioning Editor: Kate Burkett
Senior Editor: Eila Purvis
Art Direction: Evi-O.Studio | Susan Le
Design and illustrations: Evi-O.Studio | Katherine Zhang,
Typesetting: Evi-O.Studio | Matt Crawford
Food and prop stylist: Kitty Coles
Copy-editor: Caroline West
Proofreader: Esme Curtis
Indexer: Cathy Heath
Production Controller: Martina Georgieva

Colour reproduction by p2d

Printed and bound in China
by Leo Paper Products Ltd.

MIX
Paper | Supporting
responsible forestry
FSC
www.fsc.org
FSC™ C020056